D1267883

## Praise for *30 Days with Married Saints*

"One of the keys to a good Catholic marriage is praying together as a couple, and in their new book, *Thirty Days with Married Saints*, Kent and Caitlin Lasnoski have given us an incredible way to do just that. Filled with holy and devout married men and women, beautiful prayers, and intriguing discussion questions, this book is sure to bring joy and hope to married couples striving to grow closer to each other and to God."

— Karen and Tommy Tighe, authors of
*Catholic Funny Fill-ins*

"What a timely gift this book is! In it we are presented with heroes of the faith to learn from and to reflect upon. We hope it will strengthen many couples in their marriages and in their faith. Thank you Lasnoskis!"

— Kari Colella, Executive Director, Annunciation Ministries;
and Stephen Colella, Cabinet Secretary of
Parish Life, Archdiocese of Miami

"Married saints? Yes—it's possible! *Thirty Days with Married Saints* is an invitation from Kent and Caitlin Lasnoski to you and your spouse to be encouraged and inspired, together. In our ordinary lives, God can do extraordinary work in us and through us. Let's follow their lead! Highly recommended."

— Kimberly Hahn, author, *Chosen and Cherished: Biblical Wisdom for Your Marriage*

"Kent and Caitlin's book probes deep into the daily choices of married saints to reveal more of the lessons they have to teach us. Even with saints who are very familiar, Kent and Caitlin highlight new aspects, applicable to our daily lives. The Lasnoskis recount not only the dramatic acts that made these saints famous, but also the hidden heroism of daily life. As a couple, we always find that reflecting on a devotional work together enriches our relationship. These meditations on married saints' lives offer couples a practical way to enrich their spiritual bond."

— Drs. John Mortensen, President, Aquinas Institute; and Beth Mortensen, Professor of Theology, Aquinas Institute

# THIRTY DAYS WITH MARRIED SAINTS

## A CATHOLIC COUPLES' DEVOTIONAL

BY KENT AND CAITLIN LASNOSKI

FOREWORD BY JACKIE FRANCOIS ANGEL
AND BOBBY ANGEL

BOOKS & MEDIA

Boston

Library of Congress Control Number: 2019954621
CIP data is available.

ISBN 10: 0-8198-7556-2
ISBN 13: 978-0-8198-7556-3

Scripture texts in this work are taken from the *New American Bible, Revised Edition* © 2010, 1991, 1986, 1970 Confraternity of Christian Doctrine, Washington, D.C., and are used by permission of the copyright owner.

All excerpts from the English translation of the *Catechism of the Catholic Church* for use in the United States of America, copyright © 1994, United States Catholic Conference, Inc. — Libreria Editrice Vaticana. Used with permission.

Excerpts from papal and magisterium texts copyright © Libreria Editrice Vaticana. All rights reserved. Used with permission.

Franz Jägerstätter, *Letters and Writings from Prison*, ed. Erna Putz, trans. Robert A Krieg (Maryknoll, New York: Orbis Books, 2009). Reprinted with permission.

Cover design by Ryan McQuade

All rights reserved. No part of this book may be reproduced or transmitted in any form or by any means, electronic or mechanical, including photocopying, recording, or by any information storage and retrieval system, without permission in writing from the publisher.

"P" and PAULINE are registered trademarks of the Daughters of St. Paul.

Copyright © 2021, Kent and Caitlin Lasnoski

Published by Pauline Books & Media, 50 Saint Pauls Avenue, Boston, MA 02130-3491

Printed in the U.S.A.

www.pauline.org

Pauline Books & Media is the publishing house of the Daughters of St. Paul, an international congregation of women religious serving the Church with the communications media.

1 2 3 4 5 6 7 8 9                    26 25 24 23 22 21

*This book is dedicated to the holy married saints whose lives shine light on our own marital path; to our parents and grandparents whose witness of faithful love inspires us; to all married couples fervently seeking after the Lord as they journey together toward heaven; and to our children, for whom we pray and hope to make visible the love of Christ for his bride the Church.*

# Contents

# Foreword

*God cares about your love story.*

Marriage is a great adventure and a noble responsibility for those of us called by God to live this vocation. Natural marriage is the union between a man and a woman who give their lives to each other until death do them part. For the Christian, however, marriage also has a supernatural dimension. Christian married love is a sacrament, a visible sign of God's love for his beloved, the Church, the people of God. Within your marriage, therefore, God is calling you to mirror his love on earth and to encourage one another to holiness to the point where you are both transformed and actually become *saints.*

Unfortunately, we don't often hear about the married saints. Many of us think that only priests, nuns, and monks are saints, or we are rightly intimidated by the saintly life of the Holy Family: Mary, Joseph, and the God-man—Jesus himself. How could we *possibly* live up to that? Take heart. Drawing upon the humanly lived experiences of many of the married saints, including Mary and Joseph, this book will help you to see how your marriage can lead you to heaven.

The Second Vatican Council emphasized that everyone in the Church shares a universal call to holiness, which means that *all of us* are called to sanctity. What that looks like will vary radically depending on our personality, temperament, culture, and state in life. Some are called to teach, others to preach, and still others to serve. Through your marriage, you and your spouse can help bring healing to the world by the manner in which you love one another, encourage each other to holiness, and radiate that love to the world.

In the pages ahead, Cait and Kent Lasnoski pour out their love for the Lord and remind us of the beautiful dignity of the married vocation. In this book, you'll find great inspiration in the lives of the saintly men and women who have gone before us. These married saints, some of whom lived centuries ago and others much more recently, gave themselves to the Lord and bore much fruit for his kingdom. Their examples can convince you of the real possibility of glorifying God through the ups and downs of your married life. What's more, this book can help you to establish a regular prayer routine with your spouse and to start putting the lessons of the saints into action.

Through every victory and season of struggle in your marriage, know that these women and men are interceding for you.

This book will bless you. Pass it on to others.

Live your marital love boldly!

JACKIE AND BOBBY ANGEL

# Introduction

Take a moment to imagine you and your spouse in the not-too-distant future. You both have a bird's-eye view of a crowd of people, all of whom are edging forward to catch a glimpse of something. The sun shines brightly and the air is hot and heavy, but you are surrounded by a coolness. Below, tens of thousands of people cram together, but you don't feel constrained. You have been standing for hours without fatigue. In front of you towers a many-pillared basilica with a marble dome. Embracing the people as if they were the arms of God, two covered walkways curve around the square.

From a window in a building high above the crowd, a man dressed in white emerges. As he raises his arms, a hush falls over the crowded square. The man makes the Sign of the Cross and then begins to speak: "When the Son of man comes, will he find faith on earth?" (Lk 18:8). He pauses for a moment and then continues:

Dear brothers and sisters! Dear families! Today we have gathered for the beatification of a married couple . . . With this solemn ecclesial act, we intend to highlight an example of a positive reply to Christ's question. [This couple lived in] a century in which faith in Christ was harshly tried, and [yet] gave a positive reply. Even in those difficult years, this [couple], *kept the lamp of the faith burning—a lumen Christi—*and passed it on [to their children]. . . . This couple *lived married love and service to life* in the light of the Gospel and with great human intensity. Drawing on the word of God and the witness of the saints, the blessed couple *lived an ordinary life in an extraordinary way.* Among the joys and anxieties of a normal family, they knew how to live an *extraordinarily rich spiritual life.*[1]

As you may have already guessed, you are imagining the beatification ceremony for you and your spouse. The words above were taken from a homily Pope John Paul II gave at the beatification Mass for the first couple ever beatified together, Luigi and Maria Beltrame Quattrocchi. One day, God willing, such a homily might be given for you! You may think this possibility highly unrealistic and perhaps it's true that you and your spouse may never be officially canonized. But that does not mean that you cannot become saints.

In the early Church, the word "saints" referred to all Christians whether living or asleep in Christ. As Christians, we are chosen, set apart by God the Father in the Spirit as members of Christ's own Body. The indwelling of the Holy Spirit in us through Baptism makes us sharers in God's own life. Baptism sets us apart as God himself is holy and set apart. The Christian is in this world but not of this world—and in this sense, every Christian is a saint! Over time, the Church began using the term "saint" to refer to people who were officially recognized for holiness and known to be enjoying perfect union with God in heaven—the heroes, pioneers, or exemplars of the faith. Often in these early years people were declared saints by popular acclaim. They were martyrs, miracle workers, cathedral builders, founders of religious orders, defenders of important doctrines, or mystics who experienced visions, revelations, or deep union with God. As time went on, the Church prudently centralized the process of canonizing saints and extended the possibility to a greater diversity of expressions of holiness.

Canonization is more accessible to the ordinary person today. Men and women are now generally canonized when they have lived a holy life of heroic virtue and miracles are confirmed through their intercession after their death. A modern canonized saint does not necessarily have to perform miracles while alive, write the next *Summa Theologiae*, or found a monastic order. Instead, canonized saints heroically live ordinary lives as they strive to follow God's will. Of course, unless you and your spouse end up having a large impact on your local and universal church, official canonization is probably unlikely. Nevertheless, your marriage can be radically holy. A holy marriage simply involves cooperation with God's grace in life's everyday moments. Put this way, you and your spouse really can pursue great holiness in your marriage. And who knows, one day there really could be a beatification ceremony for both of you. With God's grace, anything is possible!

We hope that the vivid portraits of heroically virtuous spouses in this devotional's thirty days of reflections will inspire you and your spouse in this journey of sanctity. As you will discover, these married couples did not live picture-perfect lives. They all faced the weariness and trying times that come with every marriage. Many bravely bore the crosses of infertility, deaths of children, disease, false accusations, imprisonments, or unfaithful spouses. What characterizes them most is not merely their long-suffering in the face of evil but their joy in the good, true, and beautiful. The married saints passionately loved their spouses, delighted in their children, opened their homes to strangers, gave generously to others, and lived an intense piety. They also managed to find joy amid their day's equivalents of dirty diapers, dishes, laundry, cubicles, traffic, and office meetings.

They were the salt and light of the world and the presence of the risen Christ to those who met them (see Mt 5:13–16). Now from heaven these married saints continually intercede for the faithful's intentions, including for *your* marriage. Through their example and prayers, may the married saints lead us to Christ!

# About the Authors

Before setting sail, you deserve to know the couple that steers the ship. We are Cait and Kent, and we have been married fourteen years. We are blessed to be raising and educating eight children. Kent is the author of *Vocation to Virtue: Christian Marriage as a Consecrated Life* and has written several articles on the theology of marriage and holiness. For the last twelve years, we have designed and run marriage preparation and enrichment programs. We readily admit, however, that academic learning and professional experience does not necessarily lead to a good marriage or holy children. Though we understand our marriage to be like a bank that God uses to guide the stream of our lives toward union with him, we do not presume that our banks are strong enough to guide *you* to heaven. For this reason, we thought it would be safer (and, frankly, more exciting) to leave such a high aim to the proven example of the married saints. We hope the beautiful brushstrokes of the married saints' lives will inspire you and your spouse to entrust the palette and canvas of your marriage evermore to God. May your marriage, with the help of God's grace, become the beautiful masterpiece that he has in mind for you and your spouse.

Let's imitate the married saints.

Let's be heroic in virtue.

Let's be saints!

# All the Married Saints

# Married Saints: A Brief History

## Opening Prayer

### A Litany of Married Saints

Lord, have mercy. *Lord, have mercy.*
Christ, have mercy. *Christ, have mercy.*
Lord, have mercy. *Lord, have mercy.*
Holy Mary, spouse of Saint Joseph,
   *pray for us.*
Saint Joseph, husband of Mary,
   *pray for us.*
Holy Mary, Mother of God,
   *pray for us.*

Holy Family of Bethlehem,
  *pray for us.*
Holy Innocents,
  *pray for us.*
Holy Family of Egypt,
  *pray for us.*
Holy Family of Nazareth,
  *pray for us.*
Sorrowful Mother, in our pain,
  *pray for us.*
Saints Elizabeth and Zecharia, models of fidelity,
  *pray for us.*
Saints Anna and Joachim, grandparents of Jesus,
  *pray for us.*
Blessed Luigi and Maria Beltrame Quattrocchi, example of Christian marriage,
  *pray for us.*
Saints Isidore and Maria, protectors of farming families,
  *pray for us.*
Saint Gianna Beretta Molla, patroness of mothers and the unborn,
  *pray for us.*
Saint Margaret of Scotland, patroness of large families,
  *pray for us.*

Saint Elizabeth Ann Seton, model of hope,
  *pray for us.*
Saint Elizabeth of Hungary, patroness of those
    who suffer the loss of a child,
  *pray for us.*
Saint Monica, who rejoiced in answered prayers,
  *pray for us.*
Saints Louis and Zélie Martin, exemplars of
    holy parents,
  *pray for us.*
All you holy married saints,
  *pray for us.*
All you defenders of the family,
  *pray for us.*

When Jesus gave the Sermon on the Mount he said, "Be perfect, therefore, as your heavenly Father is perfect" (Mt. 5:48). That's a tall order! What does this mean for married couples who are struggling to live holiness amid the ups and downs of everyday life? Today we'll examine a variety of themes in the lives of the married saints. Hopefully, they will provide us with practical guidance so that we might emulate these holy couples and find holiness in our own marriages.

Interestingly, the married saints tied the knot for many reasons, not all of which included romantic love.

Many had their marriages arranged by their parents. Some entered into marriage despite a desire to remain unmarried and devote themselves entirely to God. Saint Zdislava of Lemberk, for instance, ran away to be a hermit at age seven but returned home and married in obedience to her parents. In contrast, Blessed Aleth of Dijon married at age fifteen despite her parents' ardent preference that she devote herself to religious life. Aleth had a very happy marriage and prayed that her children might enter religious life. Amazingly, all of them became priests or religious, including the great Saint Bernard of Clairvaux. Other married saints believed they had a vocation to religious life but discerned that God's will was otherwise. Blessed Elizabeth Canori Mora, for instance, wanted to become a nun but discerned that her vocation was to married life.

Many of the married saints enjoyed harmonious, loving marriages. This is true even for some of the saints who married as an act of obedience. For example, Blessed Mary of Oignies' parents forced her to marry at age fourteen to counteract her growing piety and her desire to become a nun. Despite her parents' intentions, Mary continued to live for God, and she soon convinced her husband to turn their house into a hospice for lepers. Saint Elizabeth of Hungary was sent to the royal courts of her betrothed at four years old. She married her husband, Ludwig IV, at age fourteen. Despite the arranged marriage, the couple was known for their great affection for one another. Her husband wrote, "Let people say what they will, but I say it clearly: Elizabeth is very dear to me, and I have nothing more precious on earth."[2] Another touching, if somewhat morbid, legendary story speaks to one saintly couple's affection for one another. It is said that when Saint Hilarius' wife, Saint Quieta, was buried alongside him, his arm reached up from his grave and pulled her to his heart.

Not all the married saints enjoyed harmonious relationships with their spouses. About one in ten had difficult, rocky marriages—some ending happily, others in tragedy and sadness. Saint Rita of Cascia prayed unceasingly for her unfaithful husband and eventually he repented and converted. Saint Joan of France suffered an exceptionally cruel fate at the hands of her husband, King Louis XII. When her husband was captured and imprisoned, Joan interceded to win his release. Louis later repaid her kindness by working the system to have their marriage annulled. Joan resisted but sadly accepted Rome's final decision, going on to rule a portion of the kingdom by herself and to found a religious order. Saint Homobonus, upon discovering that he and his wife were infertile, began adopting abandoned children from the streets. His querulous wife gave him no end of trouble until his patience won her over, and they worked as joyful partners to care for the orphans.

For many of the married saints, holiness was a team sport. Most saintly couples were both Christian when they married, though some had greater zeal than their spouses. Not every married saint had the support of his or her spouse. In fact, even with the support and prayers of a saintly wife or husband, some married saints had spouses who never converted. In other cases, through God's grace and fervent prayer, some spouses did eventually convert. For example, Blessed Jacopone da Todi's wife died during a public tournament when the stands collapsed. After her death, Jacopone realized that his wife had devoted herself to austere penances for the sake of his conversion. This realization helped him to change his sinful ways and dedicate his life to Christ.

The married saints were open to life, with an average of three children per couple. Like many married couples today, some saints struggled with infertility. The married saints also provide us with a much-overlooked witness, less common today, to the discerning use of sexual intimacy. Close to half of the married saints embraced periods of extended sexual abstinence during their marriages. Some abstained during certain liturgical seasons for penance and to focus on prayer, others for the sake of greater availability to do works of mercy. Even if we do not directly imitate all the worthy practices of the married saints, they teach us that intentional use of one's sexuality is a part of a life of virtue. Inspired by the example of the married saints, couples today can join the sacrifice of times of abstinence to the Cross in prayer, (such as those related to natural family planning, sickness, absence, etc.).

As is probably obvious by now, if the married saints give us an example of anything, it's how to break the mold. For this reason, the married saints can be intimidating models for our marriages. These saints are not irenic, inspiring motivational speakers who simply say, "Keep doing what you're doing, just slightly better." Instead, saints overturn conventional marriage narratives. The way of radical holiness does not typically lead to a comfortable retirement, college funds, 2.5 kids, and generally accepted approaches to sexuality. Many of these saints raised children in times when half their offspring would likely die before adulthood. They also dedicated much of their lives to works of mercy. Inspired by the full force of the Gospel, the married saints' lives defy typical success narratives and social expectations.

Precisely because the married saints lived quite varied lives, all married couples can look to them for inspiration. The ways these couples responded to infertility can encourage us all to more radically embrace spiritual fertility. By observing how these saints handled discordant spousal relationships—often with perseverance, forgiveness, prayer, patience, and especially courage—we too can make efforts in our own marriage to avoid the plague of divorce. We can also find inspiration to live more radical hospitality by observing how the married saints opened their homes to the less fortunate. Finally, though most of us do not have an arranged marriage, the married saints in these circumstances can still inspire us to embrace God's plan for family's life, even when it conflicts with our own personal plans. The details vary, but all of the married saints dedicated themselves completely to God and lived lives full of adventure, risk, sorrow, and joy. Such are the lives of the married saints. Such, we pray, may be our own.

*All the married saints, pray for us!*

## Spiritual Practice

1. What stood out to you as the main differences between the lives of the married saints and those of other familiar, unmarried saints? Which details of the married saints' lives surprised you?

2. As you read the reflection for today, did you hear God calling you to think differently about what holiness might mean for your marriage?

3. Commit to one way of thinking differently about God's call to holiness in your married life. Think of one or two practical ways that this might change your everyday decisions and perceptions.

## Closing Prayer

Lord, we pray for the grace to hear God's call in our marriage and to follow your will more closely, wherever it may lead. Amen.

# The Holy Family

*First Century*

# Joseph, a Just Man Who Listened to God

## Opening Prayer

### Litany of Humility

O Jesus! meek and humble of heart, *hear me.*
From the desire of being esteemed,
> *deliver me, Jesus.*

From the desire of being loved . . .

From the desire of being extolled . . .

From the desire of being honored . . .

From the desire of being praised . . .

From the desire of being preferred to others . . .

From the desire of being consulted . . .
From the desire of being approved . . .
From the fear of being humiliated . . .
From the fear of being despised . . .
From the fear of suffering rebukes . . .
From the fear of being calumniated . . .
From the fear of being forgotten . . .
From the fear of being ridiculed . . .
From the fear of being wronged . . .
From the fear of being suspected . . .
That others may be loved more than I,

    *Jesus, grant me the grace to desire it.*

That others may be esteemed more than I . . .
That, in the opinion of the world, others may
    increase and I may decrease . . .
That others may be chosen and I set aside . . .
That others may be praised and I unnoticed . . .
That others may be preferred to me in everything . . .
That others may become holier than I, provided
    that I may become as holy as I should . . .

Men who model healthy Christian masculinity are in short supply these days. When a man decides to follow Christ closely, too often he's left thinking that he has to check his masculinity at the door. This ideal of the "nice guy" Christian is not only mistaken, it's also contrary to God's plan. Take Adam at the time of the Fall, for example. Scripture explicitly states that Adam was with Eve when she ate the fruit from the tree (see Gn 3:6). Yet Adam remained silent. Instead of standing up and protecting Eve from the serpent's wiles, he did nothing. What's worse, he did the "nice" thing and accepted the fruit Eve offered him, even though he knew God had forbidden it. Maybe he was too busy watching Eden's version of a football game and couldn't be bothered! Saint Joseph most just and chaste is a shocking alternative to the nice guy model of Christian masculinity. Joseph's example of holy masculinity can inspire husbands to imitate him and to lead their families with a gentleness that can only come from profound strength. Today we will examine how Joseph can inspire married couples to be just and to listen to God.

In the Gospel of Matthew, Joseph is described as "a just man" (1:19). First and foremost, Joseph is just in his silent obedience to God's will. Justice is the virtue of giving both God and neighbor what they deserve. Giving God what he deserves involves worship more than anything. Joseph most just, therefore, is a man of worship and total devotion. To be just often also demands emotional discipline, a constant will, and rational discernment. Unfortunately, it's often much easier to play favorites, fold, or judge a situation through the lens of sentimentalism, a great weakness today. Sentimentalism is absent, however, in Joseph's response to Mary's pregnancy.

Some Church Fathers characterize Joseph as a just man who, in response to Mary's pregnancy, followed the law and sought to end the marriage while also mercifully refused to expose her publicly. Others believed Joseph did not want to marry because he thought himself unworthy of a wife who was "with child through the holy Spirit" (Mt 1:18). Either way, Joseph's decision was just. Pope Benedict XVI once wrote that Joseph sought in his situation to apply the law in union with love. Joseph's gentle mercy came from a place of deep power and strength. In truth, only the strong can be gentle because gentleness is the moderation of power. Someone who is weak has no power to moderate him or herself.

In addition to being just in the face of difficult circumstances, Joseph was a man who listened to God. Joseph, the guardian of Jesus—our salvation—led his family wherever God led him. The Gospels recount how God often directed Joseph through his dreams. For example, an angel appeared to Joseph in a dream and told him, "Joseph, son of David, do not be afraid to take Mary your wife into your home. For it is through the holy Spirit that this child has been conceived in her" (Mt

1:20). After the birth of Jesus, an angel appeared to Joseph again in a dream and told him to take Mary and the child and flee to Egypt to escape Herod's murderous wrath (see Mt 2:13). A third time, an angel appeared in a dream and told Joseph it was safe to return home because of Herod's death (see Mt 2:19–20). Each time Joseph heard God's messages, he discovered they demanded a difficult response. In the first case, he made himself subject to public derision by following God's instructions. In the second, he and his family became refugees, fleeing to a foreign, dangerous land. And in the third, they had to return home to an uncertain future. Scripture does not reveal Joseph's conversations with Mary after each of his dreams. But it's unlikely that Joseph was pushy or anxious. Rather, he probably related his dreams to Mary with gentle confidence in God's providence over their lives. His serene trust in God must have encouraged and strengthened Mary.

Together with Mary, Joseph was also the first guardian of the unique revelation of the mystery of God's love in Christ. In our own households, we too have a duty to guard and protect any children we might have and to raise them justly to love God. This is not always easy. For example, in our family we work to instill habits of consistent spiritual practices. We've found that it takes an extraordinary amount of energy to get a single two-year old, let alone eight children, to engage meaningfully in morning prayer! Justice requires that we remain strong to our commitment to prayer, yet gentle—despite the inevitable milk spills and cereal in our hair. Likewise, it can require great strength for couples to honor Sunday as the Lord's Day, a time to listen closely to God in the Mass and to give time for holy leisure—especially with ever-present work demands. Amid difficult family situations and tough choices, we can be inspired by Joseph's quiet perseverance and faithfulness to God's call.

*Saint Joseph, pray for us!*

## Spiritual Practice

1. Consider how you might better imitate Joseph's justice. How have you been avoiding giving God all that he deserves? All that the neighbor deserves?

2. Saint Joseph's life shows us that what our spouses most deserve is love, a love that doesn't stingily count the cost. Do you always give your spouse all he or she deserves? In what ways could you improve?

3. Make a concrete resolution to show your spouse love today in a way that you have not recently.

# Closing Prayer

Lord, we pray for the grace to be just, to hear your voice, and to be gentle leaders like Saint Joseph. We also ask for the courage to follow God's call in our marriage and to not be afraid. Help us both to guard the mystery of love in our marriage. Amen.

# Mary, Mother of Grace

## Opening Prayer

### Prayer to Mary, Mother of Grace

It becomes you to be mindful of us, as you stand near him who granted you all graces, for you are the Mother of God and our Queen. Help us for the sake of the King, the Lord God and Master who was born of you. For this reason, you are called full of grace. Remember us, most holy Virgin, and bestow on us gifts from the riches of your graces, Virgin full of graces.

*Saint Athanasius*

The modern wife often manages to take care of kids, do a great deal of the housework, and sometimes work outside the home as well. Strong, competent, and independent, the modern woman seems able to do it all. But is this what it takes to model one's life after the Blessed Mother, the holiest of all married saints? Certainly, the Blessed Mother was strong and capable. But she also was something more important—a grace-filled person. Today we will explore some ways that Mary's life demonstrates for married couples how they can bring grace to their families and to the world through a firm and continual "yes" to God's will.

According to the *Catechism of the Catholic Church*, grace is "favor, the free and undeserved help that God gives us to respond to his call to become children of God, adoptive sons, partakers of the divine nature and of eternal life" (no. 1996). Mary was made full of grace by God at the moment of her Immaculate Conception. Then, with her *fiat*, her acceptance of God's will, Mary accepted the call to bear the Son of God. As Queen of Heaven, Mary is our mother in the order of grace because she intercedes to her Son for the world's needs. In his encyclical, *Iucunda Semper Expectatione*, Pope Leo XIII explained her special role in the order of grace, "The recourse we have to Mary in prayer follows upon the office she continuously fills by the side of the throne of

God as Mediatrix of Divine grace."[3] Just as Christ's grace flows to us through the sacraments of the Church, grace from Christ flows through his Mother, the model of the Church, to us.

Certainly, Mary has an irreplaceable role in salvation history. Like her, we too can be conduits of grace in the world. One way that married couples can bring grace to those around them is by imitating Mary's acceptance of difficult circumstances. When Mary was close to nine months' pregnant, she left on a donkey for a multiday trip to a place she'd never been. She went because Joseph was returning home for the census. God's will be done. When Mary was in labor, there was no cozy birth suite and tub, no clean room, and not even a bed. She gave birth in a cave with animals—it was all Joseph could find! God's will be done. After Mary had given birth to Jesus, she couldn't show off her baby to her parents, but instead her family fled in the middle of the night to a foreign land—because Joseph had a dream. God's will be done. Because Mary recognized and trusted that she was a child of a loving God, she could accept God's will in her life, even when it was difficult. Mary's trust and steadfast joy in the face of trial showed her husband and all those around her the power of God's grace. We too are called to share the goodness of God's grace directly with others. But we can also share the goodness of God's grace indirectly, by trusting and abandoning ourselves to the loving God who guides us.

We can also imitate Mary's *Magnificat*, her hymn of praise to God in response to her cousin Elizabeth's greeting in the Gospel of Luke. After a long, dusty journey to Elizabeth and Zechariah's house, Mary could have complained about pregnancy woes, traded miraculous conception stories, or even just congratulated and encouraged her cousin. Instead, the first thing Mary does is praise the Lord in true humility. Mary's *Magnificat* shares the truth of God's mercy and grace not just with Elizabeth, but through the message of the Gospel, with the whole world. This part of the beautiful hymn praises God for Mary's role in salvation history:

> My soul proclaims the greatness of the Lord;
>> my spirit rejoices in God my savior.
> For he has looked upon his handmaid's lowliness;
>> behold, from now on will all ages call me blessed.
> The Mighty One has done great things for me,
>> and holy is his name. (Lk 1:46–49)

Notice how Mary does not praise herself but only God. She recognizes that in her smallness and weakness, God did great things for her. Her words must have prompted Elizabeth to recognize that she too was a daughter of a good and merciful God. Mary's words can also inspire us to believe that God can do great things through our marriages.

We have found a real joy by integrating Mary's *Magnificat* into our family life, through example but also explicitly. For instance, after the birth of our youngest daughter, our children gathered around her and together we prayed the *Magnificat*. Mary's words of praise elevated this special moment with a sense of purpose and joy. Granted, praising God like Mary isn't always this easy. Sometimes it's much easier to pat ourselves on the back or to just say "thank you" when someone shows us appreciation. Even for those who work in Catholic parishes or institutions, it can feel awkward to praise God's goodness when something good happens. Joyful praise can be easy sometimes or it can also require purposeful effort. Either way, we are called to imitate Mary's example whenever possible. Whether as intercessors to the Father, or models of abandonment to God's will, or encouraging examples of praise for God, we can all imitate Mary, full of grace.

*Mary, our Mother and Queen, pray for us!*

## Spiritual Practice

1. Do you consider yourself successful, both individually and as a couple? Make a list of the things in your life that make you successful.

2. How many of the items on your list follow Mary's example and involve bringing God's grace to each other, to your children, to the world?

3. What are some concrete ways that you could try to reshape the way you think and act in order to better bring God's grace to the world?

## Closing Prayer

Heavenly Father, we pray for a better understanding of the gift of your grace. Please help us to be more grateful for the grace we receive in the sacraments and may we always recognize your invitations to us to bring your grace to the world. Amen.

# Extraordinary Family, Ordinary Problems

## Opening Prayer

### Psalm 22

My God, my God, why have you abandoned me?
  Why so far from my call for help,
  from my cries of anguish?
Dogs surround me;
  a pack of evildoers closes in on me.
They have pierced my hands and my feet
  I can count all my bones.
They stare at me and gloat;

they divide my garments among them;
    for my clothing they cast lots.
But you, Lord, do not stay far off;
    my strength, come quickly to help me.
Deliver my soul from the sword,
    my life from the grip of the dog.
Save me from the lion's mouth,
    my poor life from the horns of wild bulls.
Then I will proclaim your name to my brethren;
    in the assembly I will praise you:
"You who fear the Lord, give praise!
    All descendants of Jacob, give honor;
    show reverence, all descendants of Israel!"
    (vv.1–2; 17–24)

Having just reflected on the life of Mary, the immaculate, sinless bride of the Holy Spirit and Mother of God, some of you might be thinking, "It's time to get off the bus. I can't possibly be this perfect!" Such a response is understandable, but it does miss an important detail: while Joseph was most just and chaste, and Mary was free from all sin, the world they lived in was just as messy, dirty, broken, and full of problems as our own. We shouldn't assume our lives are that much different from theirs. Today we will look at some ways that the Holy Family is more relatable than we might think.

Let's imagine an all-too-common event in married life. You're in the checkout line at the grocery store with three kids. As you put your credit card back in your wallet, you see only two of your children: one glomming on to your leg, the other in the cart. *"But where's Johnny?"* you think, feeling frantic. You try not to get worried yet. *"He's probably with his Dad at the nearby coffee shop begging for a blended lemonade."* Just then your husband returns with a latte but no Johnny in tow. You exclaim, "Where's our son?" Your husband's eyes widen as he blurts out, "I thought he was with you." Great! Johnny's gone missing. Again. A search of the store begins in the vegetable aisle and eventually ends in the candy section. Johnny is informing passing children of the dangers of food dyes in jelly beans. "We've been searching everywhere for you! We were worried sick!" you and your husband cry out in frustration. Johnny replies, "Well, where did you think I would be?"

You probably recall that nearly this exact situation happened to Mary and Joseph when Jesus was twelve. Only it was worse. Instead of losing their son for a few minutes inside the confines of a building, they lost their son for three days. They were already traveling home from Jerusalem when they realized Jesus was missing. Most likely full of panic, Mary and Joseph had to return to the bustling city and search for their only child. Joseph and Mary handled the situation as would most couples. At first, when they discovered that Jesus was missing, they assumed that he was with another family member. Then, when they realized that none of their relatives had him, a frantic search ensued. After three days of worry, they finally found Jesus in the Temple, the house of God.

Losing Jesus in Jerusalem was just one of many messes the Holy Family faced. This Gospel story in particular can provide married couples with a template for the marital messes, mix-ups, mistakes, and other unfortunate events that inevitably occur. The car won't start. My spouse is in a bad mood. Our insurance was cancelled. The kids are treating me disrespectfully. Potty training is a disaster! We feel frantic, look for help, and search all over for answers. But we can remember to begin how Mary and Joseph ended: by looking in the right place— the house of God. The answers to all our family problems are in prayer, the sacraments, Eucharistic Adoration, and Scripture. Peace in all difficulty is found in God and abandonment to his will.

We are called to be couples who model discipleship. Prayer offers a strong witness, not only for our children, if we have them, but for our spouse and those around us. One of the best pieces of advice we received in our marriage was to spend *ten times* more time praying for our children than disciplining them. Imagine, in a moment of stress, your child or spouse hears you ask the Holy Spirit for aid. Or a son happens to see his father praying a Morning Offering as he kneels before a crucifix. Or a daughter overhears her mother say she is fasting from coffee as a prayer for her children. In gardening, more time is spent preparing the soil than sowing the seeds. The same is true when raising our children or when trying to be a prayerful example for a spouse. Every moment we spend sowing the seed of virtue for our family must be prepared for with prayer on behalf of those we love. We will face struggles as we try to live for Christ and communicate the Gospel to those around us. But we can also bring any problems we encounter to the Holy Family. Mary and Joseph understand what we are going through because they went through many of the same struggles and perhaps some were even worse. They understand our struggles as married couples and pray for us in our trials.

*Holy Family of Jesus, Mary and Joseph, pray for us!*

## Spiritual Practice

1. Consider the incident of the finding of Jesus in the Temple. What are some similar problems or frustrations you've had as a family? How did you handle them? How might you handle those situations differently if you had a redo?

2. Read about some of the Holy Family's sufferings and unfortunate events: their time as refugees (Mt 2:13–15); the time they received both good news and bad news about their son (Lk 2:25–38); the time Mary stood at the foot of the Cross (Jn 19:25–27). How can these stories encourage your family in your own struggles?

3. Spend a few minutes talking to God about the children in your life, perhaps your own children if you have them, godchildren, or any nieces and nephews. Praise God for each child and ask him to help them to grow strong in virtue.

## Closing Prayer

Holy Family, pray that we may find peace in our daily difficulties, both big and small. Help us to imitate you in finding the answer to our biggest problems by following God's will. May you be an example to our family and intercede for us in our struggles. Amen.

# Blessed Luigi and Maria Corsini Beltrame Quattrocchi

*January 12, 1880–November 9, 1951 (Luigi)*
*June 24, 1884–August 26, 1965 (Maria)*

# The Beginning of a Journey

## Opening Prayer

"Blessed are you, O God of our ancestors;
    blessed be your name forever and ever!
Let the heavens and all your creation bless you
        forever.
You made Adam, and you made his wife Eve
    to be his helper and support;
    and from these two the human race has come.
You said, 'It is not good for the man to be alone;
    let us make him a helper like himself.'
Now, not with lust,

> but with fidelity I take this kinswoman as
>      my wife.
> Send down your mercy on me and on her,
>      and grant that we may grow old together.
> Bless us with children."

*Tobit 8:5–7*

In the introduction, you read an excerpt from Saint John Paul II's homily for the first joint beatification of Luigi Beltrame Quattrocchi and Maria Corsini Beltrame Quattrocchi, the married couple we will discuss today. Just as we learned from examining the Holy Family's life, this beatified couple teaches us that married sanctity is an attainable goal. Blessed Luigi and Maria did nothing that was particularly astonishing. Rather, as John Paul II pointed out, they "lived an ordinary life in an extraordinary way." Luigi and Maria's lives show us that striving for married holiness does not have to be like scaling a mountain or crossing a river full of dangerous rapids. Rather, it is more like walking into a familiar, inviting backyard onto which the doors of our homes already open. Today we will look at how this ordinary couple offers an extraordinary model of love for married couples today.

Maria Corsini was born in 1884 in Florence, Italy. Her household was characterized by conflict because her parents both had tempers. But Maria was always calm and diplomatic. In an attempt to pacify her parents' quarrels, when she set the table for dinner, she would place olive leaves, a sign of peace, under her parents' napkins. Luigi Beltrame was born in Catania in 1880 and raised by his aunt and uncle, the Quattrocchis. Luigi met Maria when the two were teenagers. Near the end of 1904, Luigi became quite ill. Hearing of his illness, a distraught Maria sent him a picture of the Madonna of Pompeii. The event revealed their deep care for each other and led to their marriage about a year later.

Interestingly, like many couples, this holy couple did not start out with the same level of interest in the faith. Luigi and Maria's second son, Cesare, would remember later that his father was not particularly devout in the beginning of his parents' marriage. His mother, however, began to have an impact on his father's spiritual life. Eventually, Luigi began to take his faith so seriously that Cesare would describe his parents' zeal as "a kind of race" between the two of them for spiritual growth. Every morning the couple would attend daily Mass together. Because liturgy marked the true beginning of the day for the couple, Luigi would wait to greet Maria with a "Good Morning" only after Mass had ended. Though it took time, Luigi and Maria began to see their marriage as a joint effort to reach heaven, and they encouraged one another in holiness.

Differing levels of devotion are not uncommon in marriage, especially given that a large percentage of Catholic marriages are between Catholics and non-Catholics. Even when both spouses are Catholic, couples may experience differing levels of faith commitment that can cause conflict. With the grace of God, the journey of any marriage can end in holiness and sanctity. Even if our spouse does not believe in God at all, we can strive to know, love, and serve the Lord every day and pray and gently invite our spouse to join us in our journey of faith. In these kinds of situations, we can find inspiration in the example of Maria who encouraged Luigi to follow Christ more zealously. As their life shows, a holy marriage is not characterized by immediate perfection but by simply striving for holiness.

Eventually, Luigi and Maria grew to love each other both by outward actions and by growing together in the interior life. Pope Pius XI writes in his encyclical on marriage, *Casti Connubii*, that the love of marriage "is proved by deeds." He continues,

> This outward expression of love in the home demands not only mutual help but must go further; it must have as its primary purpose that man and wife help each other day by day in forming and perfecting themselves in the interior life, so that through their partnership in life they may advance ever more and more in virtue,

and above all that they may grow in true love toward God and their neighbor.[4]

Couples in today's world can do the same. For example, a couple we recently helped through marriage preparation faced a difficult situation. The woman needed to speak a hard truth to a friend, something so serious that it was likely to compromise the friendship. Her fiancée could have stayed out of the situation or dismissed its importance, but instead he counseled his future wife, prayed with her, and encouraged her. In the end, with the support of her soon-to-be-husband, she sat down with her friend, and with God's grace everything worked out. This may seem like a trivial example, but it's small acts of love like this that make a holy marriage. Luigi and Maria's marriage shows us that marital holiness consists of simple acts of love that help a couple to grow closer to God and to one another.

## Spiritual Practice

1. When Luigi and Maria first met, Luigi hardly practiced his faith, yet now the two are beatified—as a couple. How has your faith and the practice of it changed over time since your marriage began?

2. Can you think of one concrete way your spouse has helped you to improve your spiritual life? Even if your spouse doesn't share your faith, has he or she helped you to grow in a specific virtue? In what ways has your spouse helped you to grow in love of God and neighbor? Praise God for the presence of your spouse in your life and for the way he or she lifts you up.

3. Write down one practical thing you can do regularly to encourage your spouse to grow in virtue and closer to God.

## Closing Prayer

Lord Jesus, we thank you for the gift of one another. We praise you for the ways you have helped us to grow closer to you. May we continue to encourage one another to grow in virtue. Amen.

# Taking up the Cross

## Opening Prayer

### God Alone Suffices

Let nothing disturb you.
Let nothing frighten you.
All things pass away:
God never changes.
Patience obtains all things.
One who has God lacks nothing.
God alone suffices.

*Saint Teresa of Ávila*

In the early years of their marriage, Luigi and Maria faced obstacles typical of young married couples. After their wedding, the couple lived in cramped quarters with Maria's parents and grandparents, an arrangement that must have complicated their first years as newlyweds. Luigi's frequent travel for work also was difficult for them both, but their many letters to one another were a source of consolation. The couple had three children in the first four years of marriage: Filippo, Stefania, and Cesare. In her letters to Luigi, Maria sometimes expressed frustration with the sacrifices she had to make for motherhood—not being up to date on the latest in music, theatre, and literature. When pregnant with their second child, Maria wondered how she would have the strength and energy to have another child, not to mention care for the infant once born. Today we will explore how this couple was able to joyfully live the trials of their early marriage by abandoning themselves to God's will in faith.

In 1913, Maria and Luigi rejoiced when they found out that they were expecting their fourth child. Little did they know that this pregnancy would be a great cross through which they would share in Christ's passion. In her fourth month, Maria began to hemorrhage and was diagnosed with *placenta previa*, a serious difficulty today but a terrifying and deadly diagnosis at the time. Since Maria only had a five-percent chance of survival, her doctors advised the couple to have an abortion. Knowing the risk, Luigi and Maria responded to this option with a categorical "No." The couple then turned to God in hope and trust despite the grief and hardship they were sure to face during the rest of the pregnancy. Maria was so weak that she had to remain in bed. With the likelihood of his wife's death looming, Luigi cared for their children and prepared to raise them as a widower. The holy couple, however, accepted God's will and drew closer as they entrusted their family to God. Miraculously, when Maria gave birth to their daughter, Enrichetta, both mother and baby were completely healthy.

Luigi and Maria easily could have justified aborting their baby. Without the abortion, the chances of survival for both mother and child were slim. They already had three children who would have been left without a mother. The doctors thought it the only sensible course of action. Luigi and Maria must have faced grave temptation to lose their trust in God. By resisting that temptation and instead trusting in God's providence, they accepted current and potential future crosses. Their example can inspire us to take up our own crosses in family life and to lean on the Lord for support.

Whether it's spilled milk, a two-year-old who continually bites all her siblings, a broken windshield wiper, or an unusually grumpy coworker, little things will provide opportunities for married couples to accept small crosses for the Lord. In our marriage, we have experienced many crosses, big and small. Sometimes lots of little crosses fall upon us at once and provide extra challenging opportunities for virtue. Once, we were both already feeling stressed because Cait was pregnant and a week past due. Then a serious thunderstorm hit and, amid claps of thunder and torrents of rain, Cait began to go into labor *and* our basement began to flood. As if that weren't enough, a few days later all our other children came down with the stomach flu. Between helping sick children, baling out the basement, and trying to care for the new baby, it would have been easy to despair, complain, and wonder "Why us?" Instead, by the grace of God, we tried to encourage one another and smile while accepting the crazy assortment of challenges the Lord had put before us. All marriages will face situations like this one—crosses are inevitable. In these situations, Luigi and Maria can be an example to us of the joyful hope that is possible when we embrace our crosses with Jesus by our side.

## Spiritual Practice

1. What crosses have you faced in your marriage? Did you have difficulty trusting in God's provi-

dence? How do you think you could have done better? Did you experience temptations to distrust God?

2. Can you think of any sacrifices that your marriage might face in the future? What can you do to prepare for these future crosses?

3. Think of one cross you are likely to face tomorrow. Ask for God's grace to carry that cross with peace and trust.

## Closing Prayer

Lord, we ask for your forgiveness for the times when we did not willingly take up our crosses and trust in you. Please give us the grace to accept whatever future sacrifices you see fit to place before us. Amen.

## DAY 7

# Together with Christ

## Opening Prayer

### Prayer from *The Imitation of Christ*

Lord God, holy Father, may you be blessed now and forever because whatever you will is done, and what you do is always good. Let me rejoice as your servant, not in myself, but in you, and not in anyone else, for you alone are true joy. You are my hope and my crown. You are my joy and my honor, my Lord. What do I have that has not come from you? What merit is mine? (see 1 Cor 4:7). All things are yours, both what you have given and what you have made. Amen.

*Thomas à Kempis (1379–1471)*

After Enrichetta's rather miraculous birth, Luigi and Maria settled down with their four children to live what was in many ways an ordinary middle-class life—but their efforts to live holiness produced extraordinary results. Luigi and Maria took seriously their responsibility to share their love for Jesus with their children. Their son, Cesare recalled, "There was always a supernatural, serene, and happy atmosphere in our home, but not excessively pious. No matter the issues facing us, they always resolved it by saying that it had to be appealed 'to the heavens.'"[5] Luigi's and Maria's efforts to instill faith in their children bore great fruit—three entered religious life and their youngest remained at home to care for her aging parents. Today we will look at the many ways this couple modeled holiness for their children and their community.

Luigi and Maria imbued their family life with many spiritual practices. Luigi led a family Rosary that sanctified every evening. The couple consecrated their family to the Sacred Heart of Jesus. And, as part of their devotion to Christ's ever-abundant mercy, the family made a monthly holy hour of Eucharistic Adoration on the eve of every first Friday. The couple also regularly trained their children to live for heaven, prioritizing those things "from the roof up," as they put it. Cesare remembered that when he was ten, his mother gave him a copy of the book, *The Imitation of Christ,* with the personal inscription

"Remember that Christ must be followed, if necessary, unto death."[6] Heavy words for a ten-year-old! Yet, also evidence of the importance his parents placed on heavenly things amid the ordinary events of family life.

Maria and Luigi's faith sustained and strengthened their family, which then allowed them to turn outward and share Jesus' love with others. Champions of the works of mercy, Luigi and Maria both dedicated a great deal of time to help the needy. Maria volunteered as a nurse for the Red Cross during World War I. Luigi received numerous awards for his community service, but he typically put the awards away in a bottom drawer, never to speak of them again. As a couple, Luigi and Maria volunteered in various community groups and even started a scouting group for youth from poor areas of Rome. The family home was also characterized by hospitality. Luigi and Maria loved to welcome anyone in need to dine with them. During World War II, the family home was opened to those in need and became a shelter for refugees. Luigi and Maria did not just teach their children the doctrines of the faith, they lived it in every aspect of their lives.

Perhaps most impressively and almost unbelievably, Luigi and Maria's children would later report that their parents rarely fought in front of them. Enrichetta recalled that her parents solved their problems in private, never marring the serenity of the home. While this may seem completely impossible in our own marriages, with the help of the Holy Spirit we can aspire to create a similar peace in our homes. As Christians following the example of Christ's radical forgiveness, we can take refuge in knowing that holiness in the family is not determined by the absence of quarrels but by the presence of reconciliation. In 1951, Luigi died from a heart attack. Fourteen years later, Maria joined her beloved husband.

As we have learned over the past few days, Maria and Luigi lived an ordinary life in a simple yet extraordinary way with the help of God's grace. Now, you may be thinking, how can we possibly imitate this holy couple's marriage and family life? Rather than making us feel inadequate, Maria and Luigi's marriage should inspire us. Following their example doesn't mean that we must immediately imitate their every spiritual practice and virtuous act. It's important to realize that Maria and Luigi's family life changed and improved over time. We too can take small steps toward developing our own unique family spirituality. Some families benefit greatly from an evening Rosary while others enjoy praying the Divine Mercy Chaplet together or even singing their favorite hymns. Maria and Luigi got involved in their community in ways they specifically felt called to by God. Their example can move us, individually and as couples, to always listen to

God's call to turn outward and to serve the community. In many ways a life like Maria and Luigi's is already close at hand. All we need do is use the gifts we have to serve our family and others in need. To imitate Maria and Luigi, and all the married saints for that matter, we simply can continue to do what we are already doing—with greater devotion and deeper love—all for God's glory.

*Blessed Luigi and Maria Beltrame Quattrocchi,*
*pray for us!*

## Spiritual Practice

1. Take some time to recount your own journey thus far as a couple, either by writing it down or by telling each other the story out loud. What serious trials have you faced? What are the highlights, the moments for which you are most grateful?

2. Maria and Luigi mastered everyday family life, all the while growing in faith and leading their children to Christ. How has your family life developed over the years of your marriage? What changes have most helped to lead you closer to Christ?

3. Write down one spiritual practice that Maria and Luigi instilled in their family that you would like to try in your own marriage.

# Closing Prayer

God of all Providence, we give you thanks and praise for the path we are walking as a couple, a path that we trust will ultimately be for our sanctification and your glory. Help us to always trust you and to grow closer to you in everything we face. Amen.

# Saint Isidore and Blessed Maria de la Cabeza

*c. 1070–May 15, 1130 (Isidore)*
*Died 1175 (Maria)*

# Faithful Workers of God

## Opening Prayer

### Prayer Before a Day's Work

Direct, we beg you, O Lord, our actions by your holy inspirations, and grant that we may carry them out with your gracious assistance, that every prayer and work of ours may begin always with you, and through you be happily ended. Amen.[7]

We've all heard the phrase, "Two heads are better than one." Well, when it comes to holiness it might be better to say, "Two hearts are better than one," especially two hearts entirely devoted to loving and serving

God. As we saw with Maria and Luigi Quattrocchi, two can better resist evil and spur one another to holiness, especially amid great trial. But the greatest bond between any couple is the Holy Spirit. As Scripture tells us, "Where one alone may be overcome, two together can resist. A three-ply cord is not easily broken" (Eccl 4:12). The more a couple's life orbits around God, especially in the holy sacrifice of the Mass, the more impossible it becomes for them to fly apart. The married saints we turn to today, Saint Isidore and Blessed Maria de la Cabeza, were one such couple. Bound by their unflappable commitment to hard work, these two were united especially in their love for the Presence of Jesus in the holy Eucharist. Unlike some of the other saints of their time, Isidore and Maria were not rich or powerful. They were simple farmers. Nevertheless, this couple was outstanding in holiness, and their lives show how we too can be faithful to our work, to each other, and to the Lord.

Isidore and Maria were born in late eleventh-century Spain. Like many saints from long ago, the details of their lives are scant and some accounts legendary. Nevertheless, their story still inspires. Isidore was known for the effort he put into his work as a farmer but even more so for the effort he put into his faith life. His wife, Maria Toribia, was his equal in dedication to the Lord. No one ever heard the couple scold or curse one another, and though they were poor, they always remembered those who were poorer and shared their wages with those in need. It is said that Maria always kept a pot of stew ready, as Isidore frequently brought needy people home. On one occasion the small pot miraculously fed a large group. While their life was happy, they also faced great difficulty. Maria and Isidore only had one son who died when he was very young. After his death, they devoted themselves even more to prayer and penance.

Isidore's hardworking nature earned him the trust and esteem of the owner of the land he tenant farmed. As often happens in this fallen world when someone finds favor, the other tenant farmers grew envious and tried to attack Isidore's reputation. Some of the farmers told the landowner that Isidore neglected his work in favor of attending Mass and praying. When the landowner asked Isidore about the accusation, the farmer explained that he had to first serve the Lord and then God would help him complete his work through the assistance of the holy angels. Legend has it that Isidore's employer actually witnessed the truth of Isidore's words when he saw two angels tilling the fields one day while Isidore was attending Mass.

Sometimes we may be tempted to think that our life circumstances keep us from holiness. Maybe we feel that our jobs are too disconnected from the faith, our houses too small or modest to extend Christian hospitality, or our education in the faith too meager. When we feel inadequate, we can follow the example of Saint Isidore and Maria and remain confident in the Lord's providence.

Our family recently was tested in the area of trusting in God's providence. A family with seven kids stopped by our house because they were in the neighborhood. We didn't feel ready to welcome them because our house was a mess and we had to get ready for dinner guests. But a spark of inspiration from the Holy Spirit and the smile on our son's face at the sight of his friends prompted us to invite them in. Then we all enjoyed ourselves for an hour and a half. And, you know what? Dinner was ready and the house was (almost) ready when our planned guests arrived. In similar circumstances, may we always imitate Isidore and Maria's simple trust in the Lord "who by the power at work within us is able to accomplish abundantly far more than all we can ask or imagine" (Eph 3:20).

## Spiritual Practice

1. Think of some situations when you felt tempted to put professional or domestic responsibilities above growing in communion with God. Do you ever feel like your duties, whether domestic or

professional, conflict with your desire for holiness?

2. Have you ever felt belittled or challenged professionally because of your commitment to Christ? Were you able to provide a positive witness in response? If you haven't experienced such a situation, consider how you might handle it should it happen.

3. According to the *Catechism of the Catholic Church*, "the Eucharist is the 'source and summit of the Christian life'" (1324). Saint John Paul II called it "the greatest treasure of the Church."[8] If you don't already attend daily Mass, pencil in some times in the next few weeks when you and your spouse could go together.

## Closing Prayer

Father, Giver of all good gifts, help us to remember that you are most important in our lives. Give us faith in your grace when we feel that what we have to offer is insufficient. May our work keep its proper place in our lives, and may we remain strong as a family against all temptation, whether at work or at home. Amen.

# Spousal Trust

## Opening Prayer

### A Prayer for Trust

Almighty God and Father, you told us that should even a mother forget her child, you would never forget us (see Is 49:15). Give us unfailing trust in you, Father of Lights (see Jas 1:17). May our trust in you pour over into our trust for one another in marital fidelity. May we trust each other implicitly, with our whole lives, knowing that we have given our lives to each other in service to you. May no word or deed of ours assail the armor of that trust. Help us to trust in each other and may your Spirit at work in us be strengthened every day. Amen.

Today we will pick up where we left off yesterday, with the men who accused Isidore of skipping work in favor of going to Mass. Like most men possessed by jealousy, they didn't give up after their first attempt to bring low this holy man. The next time around, Maria's faithfulness was put into question by Isidore's envious neighbors. Maria was known to visit a Marian chapel daily to pray and tend the perpetual oil lamp. Lying tongues spread spurious tales about the nature of her visits, insinuating that the true purpose was an illicit liaison with a shepherd. Similar moments of doubt inevitably arise in every marriage, even if just in little ways so today we will examine how Isidore and Maria chose to trust in the Lord and in one another in the face of these evil accusations.

When Isidore heard the accusations against his wife, he must have experienced several temptations. For one, he must have felt the temptation to strike out in defense of Maria's honor. The temptation to doubt Maria perhaps also loomed. Trusting in his wife's fidelity to her marriage vows, Isidore dismissed the rumors. Isidore's example of steadfast trust for Maria can spur us to examine how we exhibit trust in our own spouse. We don't typically need external accusers to lead us to think ill of our spouses. Perhaps the garbage didn't get taken out. Maybe the laundry hasn't been done. Or a spouse comes home late from work. What goes through our minds? Are we our spouse's first accuser? Or our spouse's first and best defender?

Appropriately, the Hebrew word "Satan" means "accuser." In the Book of Job, Satan plays this role when he stands in God's court and accuses Job of loving God only on account of his riches (see 1:6–12). Satan always stands ready to accuse each of us before God. Perhaps our spouses don't need another accuser as often as we provide one. Instead, we are called to view our spouse's actions with charity and to interpret them in the best possible light. The corollary to this, of course, is trusting that your spouse is trying to do the same. This is certainly not easy, especially in emotional situations. But in these circumstances, we can turn to God in prayer and ask for his help to see our spouse as he sees them.

Isidore also knew that the truth is its own defense. Isidore and Maria trusted that their marriage was based on Christ's love for the Church. So, they also trusted that their marriage could handle the truth. Many times, we fear that honesty will destroy our marriage, or that we must keep up a front because our spouse won't love us when we aren't perfect. But Isidore and Maria took Christ seriously when he told his disciples, "Let your 'Yes' mean 'Yes,' and your 'No' mean 'No.' Anything more is from the evil one" (Mt 5:37). It can be appealing in testy conversations to couch our statements, be cheeky, give half answers, or be sarcastic. When we don't want to be nailed down to anything, however, we avoid saying what we really mean. We understandably prefer to be able to back away from the consequences of saying "Yes" or "No." Christ, after all, was nailed down quite literally for his "Yes." Jesus was nailed to a cross because he was straightforward and faithful in his love for us and for his Father. Commitment can lead to suffering. God's grace gives us the courage to be men and women of clarity, simplicity, and trustworthiness when we say "Yes" and when we say "No."

If we are modeling our marriages after Jesus Truth, like Isidore and Maria, we can trust that being truthful will not damage our marriages but only make them stronger. Of course, this doesn't mean that we have permission to be mean or rude under the guise of honesty. That's a selfish ruse. It takes work to know what real, charitable honesty in a relationship looks like—but it's possible with God's grace! In the meantime, we can take a cue from Isidore and Maria and try to see our spouses and ourselves as works in progress. Our marriages are like construction sites of grace where, through the necessary demolition, sanding, and painting, God is always calling and equipping us to love one another.

*Saint Isidore and Blessed Maria de la Cabeza,*
*pray for us!*

# Spiritual Practice

1. Can you think of an occasion when you have played the role of accuser rather than your spouse's defender? Discuss what happened and how you both could have handled the situation more gracefully. Apologize to one another if necessary.

2. Discuss whether you see a pattern in situations when you are more likely to be unreasonably doubtful or accusatory of your spouse. How can you both work together to address these issues?

3. Consider any faults or weaknesses you may be keeping from your spouse out of fear that he or she wouldn't love you as you try to address them with the help of God's grace. Resolve to bring something you are struggling with in trust to your spouse and to confession if needed.

# Closing Prayer

Loving God, we pray for the grace to be trustworthy and to trust our spouses in times of difficulty. More than anything, help us to trust in the goodness of the Lord who united us in marriage. Transform our love for each other so that it might serve as light and inspiration for others. Amen.

# Saint Gianna Beretta Molla

*October 4, 1922–April 28, 1962*

# Surprising Sanctity

## Opening Prayer

### Saint Ignatius' Prayer of Self-Offering (*Suscipe*)

Take, Lord, and receive all my liberty,
my memory, my understanding,
    and my entire will—
all I have and possess.
You have given all to me.
To you, Lord, I return it.
All is yours; do with it what you will.
Give me only your love and your grace.
This is enough for me.

Today we turn to a twentieth-century Italian saint, Gianna Beretta Molla, who both spoke and embodied these words: "Our task is to make the truth visible in our person, to make the truth lovable, offering in ourselves an attractive and, if possible, heroic example."[9] Perhaps you already know this physician, wife, and mother's story. Many characterize Gianna's holiness in terms of how she dramatically sacrificed her own life rather than the child within her womb. The truth of her holiness, however, is a more expansive and nuanced reality. Today we hope to open a new vista on the life of this holy married saint by examining the details of her story that bear out a series of choices all the more masterful for being more mundane, all the more heroic for being humbler and more hidden.

While pregnant with her fourth child, Gianna was diagnosed with a benign uterine tumor. Given several options, Gianna chose the treatment option that protected her child most. Knowing that it would endanger her life, she decided on the surgical removal of her tumor rather than a hysterectomy. While a hysterectomy would have been morally justified under the principle of the double effect, it would have resulted in the death of her child as an unwanted side effect. So, Gianna rejected this option and throughout her pregnancy always insisted that her child's life should come first. Her brother, Ferdinando, one of the doctors who treated her, wrote that cases such as Gianna's often led to a "suture in the uterus [giving] way, with a secondary rupture of the uterus and immediate danger of death for the patient."[10] In taking the more cautious therapy while pregnant, Gianna did not know that it would necessarily cause her death. But she did know that her choice would likely have serious significance. She sensed that still more would be asked of her. During her pregnancy, Gianna reportedly said to her brother, "The greater part is yet to come."

On Good Friday, Gianna and her husband, Pietro, went to the hospital when her water broke. She was in labor for an entire night, so her doctors performed a Caesarean section. Gianna died a week later from septic peritonitis, an infection that resulted from her Caesarean section. The doctors' decision to perform the Caesarean section could have been related to Gianna's previous surgery to remove the tumor. As anticlimactic as it may sound, birth complications were what likely killed her. Nevertheless, Gianna was always willing to sacrifice her life for the sake of the baby if that were necessary. Gianna's heroism was the fruit of a lifetime of striving to do God's will, and her holiness has many aspects. Consider a bouquet of flowers. We judge its beauty not only by the bouquet's contents but by its arrangement. Similarly, the bouquet of Gianna's sainthood is constituted not so much by one choice, or one gigantic rose, but by many manifold blooms. Gianna chose to protect her child's life at all costs. She continually chose her child's life over her own, knowing full well, especially with her medical expertise, that she risked death.

Pope Paul VI once said of Saint Gianna, "[She] was a mother who, in order to give life to her baby, sacrificed her own life in deliberate immolation."[11] Immolation is what happens when something is offered as a burnt sacrifice. The pope's words recall the sacrificial offerings the ancient Israelites made to God. When they immolated an entire animal, it was in part a recognition that God is the source of all things. Pregnancy and birth also involve great sacrifice—from morning sickness, to varicose veins, to hormonal fluctuations, to continual worry about the baby, to labor itself. Every pregnancy has risks, some end in miscarriage, and many have complications. Though not all pregnant women can relate to Gianna's specific situation, many understand her desire to save her child's life, even at an increased risk to her own.

As married couples, we follow the inspiring example of Saint Gianna when we strive to accept difficult situations with peace and trust. We might even face similar situations. A friend of ours was twenty weeks pregnant when she experienced what was thought to be a placental abruption, which can kill a mother and baby in minutes.

Miraculously, the bleeding slowed down without explanation. She then spent ten arduous weeks, away from her husband and four children while her doctors used extraordinary medical means to forestall labor and speed up the child's development in utero. Our friend was willing to make this sacrifice so that she could remain pregnant long enough for her child to survive. Every day she remained pregnant, however, she risked her placenta tearing away from her uterus again with death only minutes away. Like Gianna, our friend showed a similar commitment to trust in the will of God and to care for her child's life more than for her own. May all mothers, with the grace of God and the support of their community, demonstrate Gianna's heroic character from the moment the pregnancy test shows positive.

## Spiritual Practice

1. Have you thanked your mother for the sacrifices she made for you during pregnancy? Or one of your grandmothers for giving birth to your parents? If not, or if it has been a while, consider thanking them soon! If you are unable to do so, say a prayer of thanksgiving for them.

2. Do you know any miraculous stories related to pregnancy—in your own life or in the lives of

those you know? Share one of those stories with your spouse or a friend.

3. Reflect on how each life is a miracle—God's hand is in each of our births. Take time in prayer to thank God for each person in your life. Read Psalm 139, and thank God for your own life.

## Closing Prayer

God, our Father and Creator of all life, thank you for the gift of life and the lives of our family members and friends. Help us continue to reshape the way we see sanctity so that we may see that we too are on the path to sainthood. Father, we also ask you to protect expecting mothers. Strengthen them throughout their pregnancy and help them to trust in you. Amen.

# Living the Works of Mercy

## Opening Prayer

### Daily Offering

O Jesus, through the Immaculate Heart of Mary,
I offer you my prayers, works, joys, and sufferings
of this day
for all the intentions of your Sacred Heart,
in union with the Holy Sacrifice of the Mass
throughout the world,
for the salvation of souls, the reparation of sins, the
reunion of all Christians,
and in particular for the intentions of the
Holy Father this month. Amen.

Gianna was an ordinary, middle-class woman—a daughter, a sister, a wife, and a mother—who lived not that long ago. She made a heroic choice for the health of her child, but a series of ordinary choices were what led her to make such a decision. Gianna was born on October 4, 1922, to faithful Catholic parents. She was the tenth of thirteen children and grew up in a middle-class home. Her devout upbringing led Gianna to develop a profound personal prayer life at a young age. When she was only fifteen, she wrote this powerful prayer in her private notes from a retreat: "Jesus, I promise to submit to everything that you allow to happen to me. Only let me know your will."[12] Today we will examine how the seeds of faith planted by Gianna's parents began to blossom in her teens and flourished in her later life.

Gianna's close relationship with God overflowed into service to neighbor. As a teenager and as an adult, she was involved in Catholic Action, a movement aimed at mobilizing laity to live the Gospel and serve others. She dedicated much of her free time to working with girls in the youth group at her parish and in Catholic Action. When teaching the young girls Gianna would emphasize, "We are apostles and if we want our work to be effective and not in vain, there is only one infallible method: prayer."[13] She also encouraged the girls to work diligently without expecting immediate rewards, "Let us always work generously and humbly; let us try not to look immediately for the fruits of our labor. Working not sleeping is what counts."[14] Gianna's work in her community was inextricably linked to her prayer life, and she taught this Christian way of living to those around her, both with example and words.

Gianna's forgetfulness of self and her desire to serve was further evidenced when she decided to enroll in medical school. She saw her vocation as a doctor through the lens of apostolic ministry. During this time, she wrote in her notes how she saw her role as a physician:

> Everyone in the world works in some way in the service of mankind. We physicians work directly on the human being. . . . We have opportunities that the priest does not have. Our mission is not finished when medicines are no longer effective. There is a soul to bring to God. There is Jesus who says: "He who visits a sick person helps me." This is a priestly mission! Just as the priest can touch Jesus, so too we physicians touch Jesus in the bodies of our patients: poor, young, old, children. May Jesus make himself visible in our midst. May he find many physicians who offer themselves for him.[15]

Gianna did not see her medical profession as merely a way to make money or to be successful. Instead, like everything in her life, she focused on how God was calling her to serve him and neighbor.

Jesus told his disciples that they would be judged on whether they clothed the naked, fed the hungry, sheltered the homeless, and visited the sick and imprisoned (see Mt 25:31–46). Jesus' words are guidelines for any Christian's actions in the world, and Gianna took them seriously throughout her life. This list of actions from the Gospel of Matthew—in addition to burying the dead and giving alms to the poor—has traditionally been referred to as the Corporal Works of Mercy. Tradition also includes a list of Spiritual Works of Mercy: instructing the ignorant, counseling the doubtful, admonishing the sinner, bearing wrongs patiently, forgiving injuries, comforting the sorrowful, and praying for the living and the dead. Gianna's deep love of the Lord and her close relationship to him in prayer from an early age enabled her to live deeply the Gospel call to live the Corporal and Spiritual Works of Mercy. As her cup overflowed with graces, Gianna shared God's love with those around her.

We too can imitate the Gospel pattern in Gianna's life—first, by taking seriously our own prayer lives and then by reaching out to serve God and neighbor. To jump-start our prayer lives, we can go on a retreat, begin a prayer journal, or just set aside regular times for prayer every day. Prayer is not complicated; it simply requires setting aside the time to talk to God. When our prayer lives are nourishing us, like Gianna's did, we will find more motivation and energy to serve and share God's love with the world around us. As we take time to pray, God will guide us to the service he wants to do through us in the world. If you and your spouse are unsure how to contribute to your parish and the broader community, seek advice from community members and friends— then make the time. Our family has found great joy in helping to serve a monthly community meal in our town. We pray you too can find a way to share God's goodness with those around you!

## Spiritual Practice

1. Do you perform any of the Corporal or Spiritual Works of Mercy regularly? If so, why? If not, why not? Reflect on times when you have felt your own cup was not filled enough to be able to share God's love with others. What did you do to reenergize and refocus? (Corporal Works of Mercy: To feed the hungry; to give drink to the thirsty; to clothe the naked; to shelter the homeless; to visit the sick; to visit the imprisoned; to bury the dead. Spiritual Works of Mercy: To admonish the sinner; to instruct the ignorant; to counsel the doubtful; to comfort the sorrowful; to bear wrongs patiently; to forgive injuries; to pray for the living and the dead.)

2. Discuss any experiences you've had doing the Corporal and Spiritual Works of Mercy. Which times have felt meaningful and fruitful? Have there been times when it has not felt rewarding? Do you ever find it too difficult to find some way to meaningfully serve others?

3. If you already have committed to certain works of mercy, are you doing them from a place of prayer? Consider making some time for adoration or extra prayer in front of the tabernacle in the next week.

## Closing Prayer

Jesus, in the busyness of our lives, help us to spend more time with you in prayer. We want to always put God first in our lives. Give us the grace to do this and to share your love with others through the Spiritual and Corporal Works of Mercy. Amen.

# Abandonment to God's Will

## Opening Prayer

### Prayer of Abandonment

Father,
I abandon myself into your hands,
Do with me what you will
Whatever you may do,
I thank you.
I am ready for all,
I accept all.
Let only your will be done in me,
and in all your creatures,
I wish no more than this, O Lord.

Into your hands I commend my soul.
I offer it to you,
With all the love of my heart,
For I love you,
And so need to give myself,
To surrender myself into your hands
Without reserve,
And with boundless confidence,
For you are my Father.

*Blessed Charles de Foucauld*

Gianna's willingness to abandon herself to God's will over the course of her life ultimately empowered her to make heroic choices for her child. Her surrender to God's providence was not something that came to her immediately. Rather, as it is for most of us, she learned over time to abandon herself to God's plan for her life. In both small and big choices, Gianna learned to entrust herself to the God she loved. Today we will look at several situations in her life when she searched for and accepted God's will, even when it seemed inconvenient or difficult.

Before she married, Gianna deeply desired to follow in her siblings' footsteps and become a missionary. Her sister, Mother Virginia, served as a doctor and religious sister in India. Two of her brothers, Francesco and Father

Alberto, worked to build and run a hospital in rural Brazil. Gianna desired to imitate her siblings' example because she believed they were living Christian discipleship to the fullest. Gianna also recognized, however, that her plans were not necessarily God's plans. Hoping for clarity in her vocation, she sought counsel. To her great disappointment, all her spiritual counselors advised her to remain in Italy for health reasons. Gianna chose not to pursue missionary work because she trusted in God's loving will for her life. Mother Virginia later recalled that Gianna always tried to "be of service, to take care of daily matters well, even the most insignificant or less satisfying matters; doing them well, and above all, willingly by abandoning herself to God's providence."[16] Letting go of her initial plans must have been difficult for Gianna, but she also trusted that she would find great happiness in doing God's will.

Eventually God's loving providence led Gianna to find great joy in a relationship with a young, devout engineer named Pietro Molla. The two were just acquaintances for several years until they both happened to attend a priest's first Mass in 1954. That day, Pietro had a deep sense that Gianna was meant to be his wife. Through prayerful discernment, they both concluded that marriage was God's will. Certain that she was called to marry Pietro, Gianna wrote in her notebooks:

Marriage, too, is a vocation. . . . What is a vocation? It is a gift from God: therefore it comes from God! If the gift is from God, our concern must be to know the will of God. We must set out on that path: if God wills, never forcing the door, when God wills, as God wills.[17]

During their courtship and marriage, the couple wrote many beautiful letters to one another. In her letter accepting Pietro's proposal, Gianna wrote, "I want to make you happy and be what you desire: kind, understanding, and ready for the sacrifices that life will require of us."[18] Pietro also embraced marriage as his vocation to holiness, writing in his journal, "The more I know Gianna, the more I am convinced that God could not have given me a greater gift than her love and companionship."[19]

Gianna's acceptance of God's plan may have led her away from her beloved missions, but it also led her into a loving marriage. Gianna and Pietro married on September 24, 1955. Just over a year after they wed, they joyfully welcomed their first son into the world, Pierluigi. Maria Zita and Laura were soon added to the family in quick succession. Immediately after the Baptism of each baby, Pietro would consecrate their child to Our Lady of Good Counsel and read a prayer composed by his wife. While family life was not always tranquil—Gianna answered medical calls at all hours and Pietro was busy with work and often traveled—the Mollas also made sure they took time to rest. The family would often vacation together in the mountains and take trips to Milan for concerts and plays. The bond of love this couple painstakingly developed helped them to navigate the choppy waters of the first years of marriage. At times, both Gianna and Pietro must have felt overwhelmed or a passing melancholy. But they also tried to handle their busyness with patience and tranquility—seeking the Lord's will through mental prayer, recourse to the sacraments, and by reaching out to one another through letters.

Gianna's abandonment to God's will took the form not only of a decision to marry, but also a decision to allow God to use that marriage to form her into Christ's image. During their engagement, Gianna wrote, "I ask you a favor from now on, Pietro, if you see me doing something wrong, tell me, okay?"[20] She trusted Pietro, and God's will, enough to make this very humble request. She knew that if they could surrender in trust to one another, it would also lead them both to greater abandonment to God's will. Her request also required a great deal of humility that many might find difficult to imitate.

For the sake of growth in holiness, married couples should consider imitating how Gianna surrendered herself completely in trust to God's plan for her life. Surprisingly, some of us might find it most difficult to do this in small areas rather than in large. In our own marriage, we both tried to imitate Gianna's openness to correction from her spouse. But we often found that we avoided correcting one another because we desired to avoid conflict. Upon realizing this, we resolved to remind one another to be more active in our attempts to help the other to grow in virtue. Some couples may be like us and need help correcting one another, while other couples may struggle because they angrily or impatiently correct one another too often. Each couple must strive to find a balance, but trust always is the key component. As we work together to grow in virtue, may we imitate Gianna's abandonment to the Lord through prayer, the sacraments, and open communication with our spouses.

*Saint Gianna Beretta Molla, pray for us!*

## Spiritual Practice

1. When have you had opportunities in your marriage to practice abandonment to divine providence? How may God be calling you to abandon yourself, your future, and your plans more fully to him? What would need to change in your marriage so that you could pray what Gianna wrote when she was only fifteen, "Jesus, I promise to

submit to everything that you will allow to happen to me. Only help me to know your will"? [21]

2. In your marital relationship, how do you heed God's call to help your spouse overcome his or her faults? Conversely, do you listen well when your spouse is trying to help you grow in virtue? How could you listen better? Are there ways that you could set aside pride and accept where you need to improve?

3. How well do you listen to God's will in the everyday busyness and crosses of married life? Identify one way you could take time to listen to God during your day today.

## Closing Prayer

God, please show us your plan for our lives and give us the grace to support and encourage one another as we abandon ourselves to your will. Help us to grow together in virtue with the goal of heaven always before us. May we remain close to you each moment of our lives. Amen.

# Blessed Franz Jägerstätter

*May 20, 1907–August 9, 1943*

# A Man of Conversion

## Opening Prayer

### Anima Christi

Soul of Christ, sanctify me.
Body of Christ, save me.
Blood of Christ, inebriate me.
Water from the side of Christ, wash me.
Passion of Christ, strengthen me.
O Good Jesus, hear me.
Within your wounds, hide me.
Permit me not to be separated from you.
From the wicked foe, defend me.
At the hour of my death, call me

and bid me come to you
That with your saints I may praise you
For ever and ever. Amen.

Saint Gianna's story unveiled an ordinary life lived with extraordinary holiness. Now we turn to another ordinary marriage that was suddenly thrown into a dramatic situation that called forth heroic virtue from both husband and wife. Executed as an accused enemy of his homeland, Blessed Franz Jägerstätter's life began as it ended—as a social outcast. Of all the saints and blesseds we've discussed so far, Franz's life of sin and conversion is perhaps the most multifaceted and complex. While the lives of saints often involve miraculous and sudden conversions, Franz's faith journey was gradual and included lapses and then subsequent growth. Franz's life, including the setbacks he faced, shows us how we can continually embrace conversion and God's mercy.

Born on May 20, 1907, Franz was an impoverished child born out of wedlock to a chambermaid and a farmer. Ostracized as a child from his community because of this, Franz was known to be a rowdy troublemaker. Raised by his grandmother until he was ten, Franz was adopted by his stepfather when his mother married. He worked on the family farm until the end of his teenage years and later went to work as a laborer in the mines.

While there, he questioned his faith and may have even stopped attending Mass. Three years later, Franz returned home with a motorcycle, the first in the village. The simple wholesomeness of farm life rekindled his devotion and faith and, with his pastor's help, Franz discerned that he was called to the vocation of marriage. He began a relationship intending to marry Theresia Auer. Their relationship was full of passion, such passion that the couple failed in chastity and bore a child out of wedlock. Franz always provided for their child, but, for unknown reasons, his relationship with Theresia ended in forgiveness but not marriage. After this situation, Franz could have chosen to retreat in embarrassment to a life of mediocre, blasé Catholicism or even left the Church, but his faith only grew.

Most of us can probably relate to the ups and downs in Franz's spiritual life. We might be tempted at times to think, "If I'm serious about my faith, I'll never get off course." But then we inevitably fail, in small and sometimes big ways. Maybe, like Franz in his mining days, we sleep in on a Sunday morning and miss Mass. Maybe an argument with a fellow parishioner or our parish priest tempts us to leave the Church. We might snap at our spouse when patience runs thin. Or perhaps we are viewing pornography or betraying our spouse in some other way. Franz's example shows us that though sin is a constant reality—even in the lives of the saints—it does not have the final word. Conversion and the joy of receiving God's forgiveness in confession can have the last laugh.

The grace of the sacrament of Reconciliation and the reality of God's forgiveness and mercy must have helped Franz from fleeing the Church in despair when he sinned. Like Franz and all of the married saints, when we inevitably fail to follow Jesus perfectly, we have recourse in the sacrament of Penance. In John's Gospel, Jesus instituted the sacrament when he told his apostles, "Receive the holy Spirit. Whose sins you forgive are forgiven them, and whose sins you retain are retained" (20:22–23). According to the *Catechism of the Catholic Church*, confession "makes sacramentally present Jesus' call to conversion" (*CCC* 1423). God's forgiveness and peace is given to us through this great gift. All we need do is take advantage of it. Preparing for and going to confession can be uncomfortable, but it is also spiritually refreshing. Examining our conscience to uncover our buried sin is a bit like a deep tissue massage for the soul. A prayer to the Holy Spirit can help to jog our memories, and a pencil and paper at the ready is helpful too. Reflection on the Ten Commandments can help us to look over recent events in our lives and identify ways we have failed to respond to God's grace. When we take advantage of the sacrament of Penance, we follow in the footsteps of Franz, a man who trusted in the enduring mercy of God.

In 1936, God's mercy led Franz to meet the love of his life, Franziska. A pious Catholic, Franziska would lead Franz deeper into his faith. Together, the two took their engagement very seriously and prepared for six months before marrying. After their wedding, they went on a honeymoon to Rome. With hard work and preparation, the couple formed a loving and enduring connection that helped Franz to grow even more devout in his faith. He soon became the sexton at the local parish and went to daily Mass. Within a few years, God blessed the couple with three daughters, and the family lived happily in peace. Little did they know that in a few years, however, a decisive moment would prove lifechanging. Tomorrow we will look at how Franz faced this excruciating situation with faith and trust in God.

## Spiritual Practice

1. How often do you make an examination of conscience? Take some time to make one. If you need inspiration or help, Saint Francis de Sales' *Introduction to the Devout Life* has a wonderful section that explains the importance of doing a regular examination of conscience and offers a

method. The United States Conference of Catholic Bishops (USCCB) also has a few different examinations of conscience available online.

2. If you feel comfortable, discuss with your spouse some ways you feel you have failed in love recently, especially with respect to your role as husband or wife and father or mother. Take time to listen to one another and to offer forgiveness.

3. When is the last time you went to confession? If you are hesitant, reflect on what might be causing your hesitation. Then consider making a resolution to go to confession as a couple sometime soon. If possible, get out your calendars and pencil in a date and time!

## Closing Prayer

Holy Spirit, reveal to us any blind spots or wounds that might lead us to sin and help us to have true contrition whenever we fall. Fill us with your gifts and grace as we try to avoid sin and live for heaven. Amen.

## DAY 14

# Principle in the Face of Peril

## Opening Prayer

### Prayer to Saint Michael the Archangel

Saint Michael the Archangel, defend us in the battle. Be our defense against the wickedness and deceit of the devil. May God rebuke him, we humbly pray. And you, O prince of the heavenly host, by the power of God banish into hell Satan and the other evil spirits who roam through the world seeking the ruin of souls. Amen.

*Pope Leo XIII*

*Day 14*

Franz and Franziska were happily married for almost seven years when, through a series of political events, he confronted a life-or-death choice. His ordeal began with what must have seemed to be a harmless and mundane exercise of his voting rights. In 1938, Austrians voted on the issue of whether to accept or reject the annexation of their country by Nazi Germany. Franz was the one person in his town who voted against annexation. Supporters argued, in part, that the Reich was fighting to improve the world as they conquered it. Around this time, Franz wrote in reply to this claim:

> When our Catholic missionaries went to a pagan country to make them Christians, did they advance with machine guns and bombs in order to convert and improve them? . . . If adversaries wage war on another nation, they have usually invaded the country not to improve people or even perhaps to give them something, but usually to get something for themselves.[22]

After Austria became part of the Third Reich, Franz was drafted. Obeying his conscience, he objected to the war and refused to serve.

Miraculously, an intervention from Franz's mayor twice won his release from service. In 1943, he was drafted a third and final time. When Franz was called a third time, it was clear that authorities were not going to continue to tolerate his resistance to the draft despite his offer to serve his country in a nonviolent capacity. Almost everyone Franz knew, including priest friends, attempted to convince him to serve in the military to save his life. They urged Franz to sacrifice his conscience for the sake of his wife and daughters. Franz, however, knew he could not go against his conscience without offending God. Nothing would allow him to participate in an unjust war. He preferred to risk all as a glorious witness to the truth. Rather than run from his fate, Franz presented himself at the military base at Enns on March 1, 1943, and again stated his preference to participate in some nonviolent service on behalf of his country. His status as conscientious objector was denied, and Franz was thrown in prison.

During the time Franz was imprisoned before he was tried for sedition, he wrote many letters to his beloved family. He penned these words just before his execution:

Now I'll write down a few words as they come to me from my heart. Although I am writing them with my hands in chains, this is still much better than if my will were in chains.

Not prison, not chains, and not even death are capable of separating people from the love of God, of robbing them of their faith and free will. God's power is invincible. . . .

[Some people] always want to prick my conscience concerning my responsibilities for my wife and children. . . . Did not Christ himself say that whoever loves wife, mother and children more than me is not worthy of me?[23]

At 4 p.m. on August 9, 1943, the same day he wrote the above words, Franz's death sentence from the Reich Military Court was carried out by guillotine. His final words to his suffering family were: "And now all my loved ones, be well. And do not forget me in your prayers. Keep the Commandments, and we shall see each other again soon in heaven!"[24]

Hopefully, most of us will never have to face a similar life-or-death situation. All couples, however, can prepare for peril, should it find them, by living lives of virtue. For this reason, it might help to reflect on the possibility that our own situations might be more like the Jägerstätters' than we'd like to acknowledge. Perhaps we blindly patronize businesses where workers suffer unjust working conditions and wages. Or maybe we unquestioningly consume more than we need simply because we can. Of course, there's a difference between participating in an evil act, which is always wrong, and the various ways we may indirectly cooperate with evil (which is impossible to completely avoid in today's society). We can always ask ourselves, "How is God calling us to combat evil in our daily lives?" Is he calling us to make a defiant stand against the evils of abortion and to actively support better options for women in crisis pregnancy? Are we being called to advocate vigorously for immigrants who suffer untold injustices? When we find ourselves in situations where Church teaching and our consciences inform us that we must act, we can ask Blessed Franz Jägerstätter to intercede for us. With the help of the Holy Spirit, may we respond as he did—with great courage and determination!

## Spiritual Practice

1. What principles most define your daily actions? What principles might you be ignoring for the sake of convenience or even apparent necessity? Are there areas in which you could be more prophetically principled? Make a resolution as a couple to pick one principle you share that you want to live out more radically.

2. Spend a moment reading the poem below that Franz wrote for his godson. How does it make you feel? What do you think Franz wanted his godson to understand from it?

    *Consider two things. From where? To where?*
    *Then your life will have its proper meaning.*
    *Whoever goes on a journey without a goal*
    *Wanders poor and weary.*

*Whoever lives life without a goal*
*Has flourished in vain.*

3.  After considering Franz's poem, take a moment to
    discuss with your spouse what you both think is
    the goal of your marriage, both at the general and
    the specific level. Are there areas where your mar-
    riage risks "wandering"? Resolve to bring those
    areas in line with the goal of your marital journey.

# Concluding Prayer

Lord, show us how we can live your Gospel message
more radically, even at the cost of comfort. Give us the
grace to desire to be faithful more than successful. Amen.

# Faithful Love in Letters

## Opening Prayer

### A Prayer from the First Letter of Peter

Blessed be the God and Father of our Lord Jesus Christ, who in his great mercy gave us a new birth to a living hope through the resurrection of Jesus Christ from the dead, to an inheritance that is imperishable, undefiled, and unfading, kept in heaven for you who by the power of God are safeguarded through faith, to a salvation that is ready to be revealed in the final time. In this you rejoice, although now for a little while you may have to suffer through various trials, so that the genuineness of your faith, more precious than gold that is perishable even though tested by fire, may prove to be for praise, glory, and honor at the revelation of Jesus Christ. Although you have not seen him you love him; even though you do not see him now yet believe in him, you rejoice with an indescribable and glorious joy, as you attain the goal of [your] faith, the salvation of your souls.

*1 Peter 1:3–9*

We thrive on communication with those we love, about what we love. The buzz or jingle of a text message from a spouse can trigger a spark of joy or a sense of dread. Did my favorite football team win? Is my spouse mad at me? Has my son taken his first steps? Are the kids sick? Is my wife in labor? How we choose to communicate as married couples can strengthen a marriage or destroy it. Today we will examine excerpts from letters between Franziska and Franz that were written when he was in prison. The way they strove to communicate love to one another despite their harrowing situation can serve as an inspiration for all married couples.

Throughout Franz's tortuous imprisonment up until his death, he and his wife exchanged words of encouragement. Their letters demonstrate that they both saw value in writing and speaking edifying words in order to impart grace. They did not communicate their love with flowery phrases but simply and clearly. Franziska often wrote to her husband about seemingly mundane things—the beauty of their farm, the good days (harvesting at 3 a.m.) and bad days (no rain), and the many feasts she celebrated with their children, often walking many miles to church. Franziska did not waste time complaining, likely out of love for her husband whom she wished to avoid causing further stress. Rather, she just shared the simple details of their family life to uplift her husband's spirits and show him support.

Knowing that he might not return home from prison, Franz's priority was to communicate love and encouragement to his family. He always thanked his wife and children and gave them practical suggestions to grow in devotion. In one letter Franz mentioned his gratitude for visits in prison that he received from priests so he could receive the Eucharist and he encouraged his family to make the First Friday Devotion. When Franz had been in prison for a little over a month, he wrote this letter to Franziska on April 9, 1943:

Greetings in God! Dearest Wife!

Above all, my deepest thanks for the three letters which I have received from you with great joy during this week. Despite all of the work that you have, you remain concerned to give your husband joy, which I perhaps do not deserve . . . Please forgive me for not writing to you more often, for I cannot tell you much that is new here. I have still not received a trial.

Dearest wife, it was seven years ago today that we promised each other love and faithfulness before God and the priest, and I believe that we have faithfully kept this promise. Moreover, I believe that God still confers his grace on us, even if we must live apart, so that we can be faithful to this promise until the end of our lives. When I look back and observe all the good fortune and the many graces that have come to us during these seven years, I see that many things often border on being miracles. If someone were to say to me that there is no God or God has no love for us, and, if I were to believe this, I would no longer understand what has happened to me. . . .

Dearest wife, if we should find ourselves anxious about the future, we must not forget the thought that God has preserved us and favored us and will not abandon us, and we must not grow weary of our struggle for heaven . . . While I sit now behind prison walls, I believe I can build further on your love and faithfulness.[25]

Despite Franz's suffering, deep loneliness, alienation, and maybe even doubts, he voiced not a word of complaint in this letter. Instead, he focused on his gratitude for his wife and tried to strengthen his wife's trust in God's faithfulness. Franz also expressed a confidence in Franziska's fidelity to their marriage vows that flowed from his own faith in the goodness of God.

When Franz was given yet another chance to reconsider his decision, Franziska managed a surprise visit to the prison with their pastor. During the visit, the priest counseled him to relent for the sake of his family. Soon after the meeting, Franziska encouraged her husband:

> Greetings in God, dearest husband!
>
> We decided to travel home today . . . We are with your defense attorney, and I hope that with God's help everything will be made right. I had intended to tell you so many stories about life at home, but I forgot so much. You yourself were annoyed. But the pastor meant well. I'll surely pray a great deal for you, and please do not lose heart in your difficult situation.
>
> Truly warm greetings to you from your loving wife, Fani, who is concerned about you.
>
> P.S. Also, many kisses. Be well. See you again.[26]

Franziska's simple honesty, humility, and encouragement is striking considering her circumstances. Though the day was in many ways a failure, she manages to speak words of strength and hope to her husband and to avoid trying to change his mind. Though Franziska certainly did not want her husband to die, she trusted both in his decision to follow his conscience and in his love for her and for God. At the moment of Franz's execution, Franziska would describe feeling an intense, personal communion with her beloved husband. Not even death could destroy their bond of love, an icon of God's love for his Church.

Franziska and Franz's relationship shows us that loving communication is essential in any marriage. How we speak to one another in our day-to-day lives has the power to make our marriage better or worse. Franz and Franziska's loving communication with one another embodied Saint Paul's exhortation to the Ephesians, "Let no evil talk come out of your mouths, but only what is useful for building up, as there is need, so that your words may give grace to those who hear" (Eph 4:29). When we consider how we generally choose to communicate to our spouse, it's important to remember that the same message can be conveyed in very different ways. Do we try to communicate optimism and lift our spouse up? Do we seek to share good news and not to spread harmful gossip? Do we try to encourage rather than criticize? When we struggle to be a loving presence to our spouse we can remember the example of Franz and Franziska and trust that loving communication is possible with God's grace, even in the most difficult circumstances.

*Blessed Franz Jägerstätter, pray for us!*

## Spiritual Practice

*To ensure you have adequate time for today's practice, we've limited it to one question.*

1. Saint John Chrysostom once wrote, "There is nothing which so welds our life together as the

love of man and wife." When was the last time you wrote a love letter to your spouse? Take some time to write a letter of encouragement and love to your husband or wife. Express gratitude for your spouse's love and presence in your life and try to impart words of grace to encourage your spouse to follow Christ closely.

## Closing Prayer

Father, fill us with joyful thanksgiving for the gift of one another. Give us words to edify in spite of struggles and hearts that delight in what is good and beautiful. Amen.

# Saints Henry II and Cunegund: Royal Married Saints

*May 6, 973 – July 13, 1024 (Henry)*
*c. 975 – March 3, 1040 (Cunegund)*

# Christ Enthroned

## Opening Prayer

### Te Deum

*(Christian hymn of praise dating back to the fourth century.)*

> We praise you, O God; we acknowledge you to be
>     the Lord.
> All the earth worships you, the everlasting Father.
> To you all the angels, the heavens, and all the Powers,
> the Cherubim and Seraphim cry out without ceasing:
> Holy, holy, holy Lord God of hosts!
> The majesty of your glory fills the heavens and
>     the earth.
> The glorious band of apostles,

the great company of prophets,
the white-robed army of martyrs praise you.
Throughout the world the holy Church extols you:
the Father, whose glory is without measure,
your true and only Son, worthy of total adoration,
and the Holy Spirit, the Paraclete.
You, O Christ, are the King of glory.
You are the eternal Son of the Father.
You did not spurn a virgin's womb to redeem
      mankind.
You overcame death, and opened the kingdom
      of heaven to all those who believe.
Now you are seated at the right hand of God, in the
      glory of the Father.
We believe that you will come again as our judge.
Help your servants, whom you have redeemed
      with your precious blood.
Number them among your saints in everlasting glory.
Save your people, O Lord, and bless your inheritance.
Govern them, and keep them safe forever.
Through each day we bless you
and praise your name forever; indeed, forever
      and ever.
Grant, O Lord, to keep us without sin this day.
Have mercy on us, O Lord; have mercy on us.
Let your mercy be upon us, O Lord, as we place
      our trust in you.

> In your mercy, O Lord, I have trusted; let not my
> trust be in vain.

For the next three days we will look at some married saints who led lives quite different from our own. (Unless your three-year-old daughter doesn't just playact as a princess and has some actual royal blood!) These saints' stories will likely vary from our own in many ways, including in wealth, power, prestige, and the difficult decisions they had to make, which shaped nation and Church. But these kings and queens are also similar to us in one very important way: they were married. For this reason, though they lived in vastly different times and circumstances, we can learn from these married saints how to overcome many of the same trials couples face today.

Today we begin with Saints Henry II and Cunegund. Born around the year 973, Henry II was educated with the intention that he would become a priest. His teachers included the holy bishop Saint Wolfgang. Henry's wife, Cunegund, was the daughter of a count and the sixth of eleven children. She, too, was gifted with a thorough education. After their wedding, quite unexpectedly, Henry became king and thus Cunegund queen—first of Germany, then Italy, and finally the couple became emperor and empress of the Holy Roman Empire, a feudal monarchy that encompassed much of present-day Europe at the start of the early modern centuries. This holy couple took their duties seriously and ruled together. Cunegund would often represent Henry at various occasions, advise him, and carry out the duties of imperial administrator.

Henry and Cunegund were truly a medieval "power couple," achieving a great many things. Sadly, they were unable to succeed in the one thing most paramount for a couple in their position: bearing a successor. The royal couple was happy but remained childless. Some speculation has been made that their childlessness stemmed from a vow of virginity Cunegund made before marriage, but historians now give little credence to the claim. Today infertility issues would not necessarily lead to the dissolution of a marriage. But at that time, kings in this situation often turned to divorce to rectify childlessness. Henry was likely tempted to divorce his wife in order to produce an heir. His dynasty, his family, and his advisors must have pressured him to find another wife, but he remained faithful to the promises he had made to his wife. Henry and Cunegund remained married until his death.

Henry and Cunegund's example demonstrates the truth that a holy marriage can be immensely fruitful even when a couple suffers the cross of infertility. Making Christ the ruler of their marriage, Henry and Cunegund ultimately allowed him to define the manner of fruitfulness in their marriage. Thus, though they had no children, they treated the Body of Christ as their heir. The king and queen gave generously to the Church, donating land for new dioceses and funds to build churches and monasteries.

Couples who suffer from infertility can be inspired by Henry and Cunegund's example of marital fruitfulness despite their lack of children. While married couples are called to be open to biological fruitfulness as a gift from God, we also should be attentive to the ways God calls beyond biological fruitfulness. Adoption, fostering, or sponsoring a child are obvious ways some couples can live fruitfulness. One family we know not only adopted two children, but they also generously help other families as much as possible. Once, our family was in the middle of packing for a cross-country move when we lost power for a week because of a terrible storm. Our friends not only showed up with a generator, but they also watched our six children so we could focus on packing. No matter the number of children a married couple might have, all married couples are called to the fruitfulness of sharing God's love. In whatever way God calls us to marital fruitfulness, may Saints Henry II and Cunegund's example encourage us to enthrone Christ in our lives.

*Saints Henry II and Cunegund, pray for us!*

# Spiritual Practice

1. As a couple what do you tend to prioritize over Jesus? Discuss some ways you could give Christ supreme rule over your marriage.

2. Have you ever been tempted to be unfaithful to your spouse? Fidelity in marriage can be betrayed on many levels: sexual, time, money, charity, and thought. Have you ever yielded to temptation in any of these ways? After praying about this individually, talk with your spouse and ask for forgiveness for times you've failed. Pray together and consider going to confession to receive forgiveness and healing from the Lord.

3. Is Christ calling you to expand the fruitfulness of your marriage? Perhaps you feel called to host a Bible study at your parish, your home, or even your workplace. Or you might feel a call to volunteer to help clean your parish or to donate an item needed for worship. If you feel the Holy Spirit calling you to something in particular, consider making a resolution to pursue it.

# Closing Prayer

Jesus, give us the grace to remain faithful to one another in all things. Help us to see where you are calling us to greater fruitfulness in our marriage so that we might share your love with the world in new ways. Amen.

# Blessed Gisela and Saint Stephen of Hungary

*985 – 7 May 1065 (Gisela)*
*c. 975 – 15 August 1038 (Stephen)*

# Evangelism by Example

## Opening Prayer

### Prayer to Witness to the Gospel

Jesus, Word of God, you said, "Go, therefore, and make disciples of all nations, baptizing them in the name of the Father, and of the Son, and of the holy Spirit, teaching them to observe all that I have commanded you. And behold, I am with you always, until the end of the age." (Mt 28:19–20). Give us the strength to share your good news by word and deed, that all we meet might be invited and inspired to become your disciples and walk more closely with you.

Blessed Gisela, Saint Stephen, and their son, Saint Emeric, helped prepare the way for the conversion of the Hungarian people by steadfastly living their Christian faith. When the eyes of their nation were upon them, this family strove to live exemplary Christian piety. Inspired by the Holy Spirit, they laid the groundwork necessary, by their actions and examples, to convert the pagan nation of Hungary to Christianity.

Gisela was born and raised in a devout Christian family. Yesterday, we discussed her saintly brother, Henry II. Like her brother, Gisela was well educated in Christian truths and virtue. She was married to her husband, Stephen, when she was only about eleven. Stephen, who was around fifteen years her elder, was born with the name Vaik into the Árpád dynasty of Hungary—a dynasty formerly closed off to Christianity's influence. His mother and father are said to have converted, allowing him to be baptized and given a Christian name. Stephen's date of baptism is unknown, but it may have been in his early teens, a key time for the seeds of faith to take root. Stephen approached the faith with devotion and rigor, committing himself to live according to Christian principles. He was educated by the holy bishop, Saint Adalbert of Prague.

Together Gisela and Stephen strove to bring true Christianity to the Hungarian lands. They founded the first diocese in Veszprém and went on to organize others. They also built several monasteries and schools for the education of priests and teachers. Eventually, Stephen gained the official favor of Rome against his pagan rivals and he was crowned apostolic king. That achievement further motivated Gisela and Stephen to live as holy Christian examples for their people. Their one son, Emeric, was given a strict, no-frills education with the holy bishop Saint Gerard of Csanád. Certainly in part due to Gisela and Stephen's pious upbringing, Emeric would become known as a man of supreme virtue and magnanimity. United in their desire to be virtuous models for their people, this family helped one another to grow in holiness.

Unlike many kings who grow jealous of their sons as they mature in wisdom and favor with the people, Stephen elected Emeric to be coregent during his own lifetime. The hope was that father and son would rule together, with Gisela helping, advising, and encouraging them. Unfortunately, just before his coronation, Emeric was killed by a wild boar. A few years later, Stephen also died, leaving Gisela at the mercy of the pagan princes of Hungary. They did not treat her kindly. She was imprisoned, but eventually King Henry III freed her and she entered into a convent. Recognized for her holiness, Gisela later was elected as abbess and spent the rest of her days in the convent.

Gisela, Stephen, and their son Emeric modeled their lives after the Holy Family. Undoubtedly, one of the things Mary and Joseph took great pains to teach the Child Jesus was religious devotion and Scripture. If a couple's marriage is blessed with children, Gisela and Stephen's example reveals the fruit that can be borne by putting a child's faith education first. The *Catechism of the Catholic Church* teaches that parents have a right and duty to give their children a Christian education:

> As those first responsible for the education of their children, parents have the right to *choose a school* for them which corresponds to their own convictions. This right is fundamental. As far as possible parents have the duty of choosing schools that will best help them in their task as Christian educators. Public authorities have the duty of guaranteeing this parental right and of ensuring the concrete conditions for its exercise (*CCC* 2229).

Keeping the word of God and Christ-centered religious practice at the center of a child's education is a serious challenge, but one that is possible with God's grace.

In our own marriage, we have discerned that it would be best to homeschool our children. With no Catholic schools in our city, we decided to teach our children ourselves in order to keep Christ at the center of their education. This decision was not easy for us as it meant finding a way to live on one income. We had to shift work schedules so both of us could participate in our children's schooling. We also have tried to keep in mind that the most fundamental, powerful education we can provide for our children is a virtuous, loving example. This power can become visible in a family both with a parent's successes and failures. As a parent, there's nothing more troubling than seeing children imitate a parent's vice. Then again, there's no experience so glorious as seeing children imitate a virtue that a married couple has prayed for the grace to develop and model. Regardless of whether we have children, may Blessed Gisela and Saint Stephen's example help us to become mirrors of the Holy Family's self-giving love.

*Blessed Gisela, Saint Stephen, and Saint Emeric,*
*pray for us!*

# Spiritual Practice

1. According to the *Catechism of the Catholic Church*, "A virtue is an habitual and firm disposition to do the good" (no. 1803). Share with your spouse the virtues in which he or she excels. You might consider the four natural or "cardinal" virtues of prudence, justice, temperance, and fortitude; or the theological or "supernatural" virtues of faith,

hope, and love. If applicable, discuss the virtues of each of your children.

2. How are your virtues as a couple an example to those around you—at home, at work, at church, etc.? Consider which virtues you may need to develop to set a better Christian example.

3. Resolve to work on one virtue and help one another to grow in it.

## Closing Prayer

Heavenly Father, support us with your grace as we seek to grow in virtue. Help us to see the ways in which we might become a better Christian example of family life. May you continually transform our family to be more like that of the Holy Family. Amen.

# Saint Elizabeth of Portugal

*1271–July 4, 1336*

# A Royal Peacemaker

## Opening Prayer

### Peace Prayer

Lord, make me an instrument of your peace.
Where there is hatred, let me sow love;
where there is injury, pardon;
where there is doubt, faith;
where there is despair, hope;
where there is darkness, light;
and where there is sadness, joy.
O Divine Master, grant that I may not so much seek
    to be consoled as to console,
to be understood as to understand,

to be loved as to love.

For it is in giving that we receive,

it is in pardoning that we are pardoned,

and it is in dying that we are born to eternal life.

Jesus tells us, "Blessed are the peacemakers, for they will be called children of God" (Mt 5:9). Today's married saint, Elizabeth of Portugal, was known as a peacemaker. Born in Spain in 1277, she was given her name at Baptism, after her saintly great-aunt Elizabeth of Hungary. The joy of Elizabeth's birth calmed a feud between her father, Peter III, the future king of Aragon, Spain, and his father, the reigning king. Elizabeth would prove to be a true peacemaker not just at her birth but throughout her life and even at her death: forgiving, turning the other cheek, seeking resolutions, alleviating discord, and bringing disputes to reconciliation.

At age twelve, Elizabeth was married for political reasons to King Denis of Portugal. Eight years after their marriage, she and Denis had two children, a daughter and a son. Unfortunately, Denis also took many mistresses and fathered at least seven children with other women. When Denis insisted that these children live at the palace, Elizabeth chose to welcome her husband's children as if they were her own and raise them according to Christian principles. Through many years of her husband's infidelity, Elizabeth must have experienced a great deal of bitterness and anger as she could do little to protest his power and immoral choices. She chose, however, to bring peace to her household through the graceful way she handled Denis' callous behavior. Elizabeth also did all she could to open a way for conversion in her husband; she even undertook severe penances for his sins. When Denis fell ill in 1324, Elizabeth lovingly cared for him. Before he died, the queen's fervent prayers were answered, and the king repented for his sins.

Known as the "Angel of Peace," Elizabeth's reputation as a peacemaker extended beyond the realm of the palace. Time after time, Elizabeth poured the water of God's grace and peace on the raging fires of sin that sought to tear apart her feuding family. Before her husband's death, she brought peace to a dispute between her spouse and his brother by giving her brother-in-law an estate from her own possessions. When her son, Alfonso, took up arms against his father out of jealousy for the special attention he paid to his sons fathered with other women, Elizabeth actually rode onto the battlefield to prevent violence. Physically placing herself between the two warring sides, she convinced them to abandon their dispute.

Upon the death of her husband, Elizabeth spent her last days living as a Franciscan tertiary near a Poor Clare monastery she had founded. She left this convent one final time to attempt to restore peace between her son, Alfonso, and her son-in-law, Ferdinand IV. As word spread that Queen Elizabeth was rushing to the battlefield in the oppressive summer heat, the two sides ceased their fighting. Unfortunately, the commotion and the extreme weather were too much for Elizabeth. She developed a high fever and died in the arms of her son and daughter-in-law.

We don't know about your family, but ours certainly isn't a picture-perfect portrait of peace. While land and power struggles are not usually what tear our family apart, building blocks all over the floor and hair-pulling certainly do. Regardless, the source of all family feuding is the same: sin. All families can have hope because the cure for all feuding also is the same—Jesus! As we try to bring peace to our children's quibbles and sometimes even to extended family drama, we can turn to Jesus for help in bringing peace to those around us. We are also called to bring peace in the face of inevitable spousal conflicts. Resolution of conflicts with our spouse necessitates the courage to communicate honestly and charitably. We may not be called to the levels of Elizabeth's boldness—by physically stepping into the middle of an argument—but we will certainly need to be willing to raise uncomfortable topics. Peace in marriage involves both gently calling our spouses to account *and* admitting our own failings.

As we saw in Elizabeth's marriage with her husband Denis, infidelity of any kind cuts deeply and causes conflict in any marriage. Reconciliation in these instances is not always possible. We know one couple who experienced the reality and sin of infidelity on the part of one spouse and still, their marriage was able to recover. This marriage was able to rise from the ashes of betrayal through the mighty witness of conversion and the grace of forgiveness. In this situation, one spouse's radical witness of Christian forgiveness and invitation to conversion and reconciliation made all the difference. After the incident, the couple gradually started walking closer with the Lord. As a result of their journey, they have been able to share with many couples over the years how God worked in their marriage, helping other couples prepare for their own marriages. Whether a couple experiences sexual infidelity or infidelity of another kind (time, energy, etc.), one thing is certain: all couples are called to continual conversion and to regular prayer for one another. Saint Elizabeth of Portugal's life shows us that prayer is one of the most powerful ways to bring peace. Through her intercession, may Jesus bring peace to our families and to the world.

*Saint Elizabeth of Portugal, pray for us!*

# Spiritual Practice

1. Read the Beatitudes (see Mt 5:1–12). Discuss whether you especially identify with or feel called to live any of the passages.

2. Take turns sharing with your spouse how you feel he or she brings peace, forgiveness, and love to others and to your marriage. How could you both be a more peaceful presence to those around you?

3. Are there particular situations within your family, friends, or in the wider community in which you feel called to act as a peacemaker? Make concrete resolutions to take steps toward peace in one or two relationships in your life.

# Closing Prayer

Lord, through your grace, make us instruments of your peace. Bring peace to our homes, our Church, our workplaces, our country, and our world. Amen.

# Blessed Frédéric Ozanam

*April 23, 1813–September 8, 1853*

# DAY 19

# Faith in Action

## Opening Prayer

Heavenly Father, you love each of us with an unending love that can never be equaled but that we should always strive to imitate. Help us to model your love for others by caring and praying for all those in need that you put in our paths. Help us also to seek out ways to share your love with those in need. May we always find our strength in your love. And from that place of security and joy, help us to go out into the world as your instruments of love. Amen.

Most of us probably typically respond to a person sharing a problem by saying, "I'll pray for you." On the one hand, this excellent response deserves praise because prayer carries more power than a nuclear reaction. On the other hand, sometimes we forget that it's also important to respond to the needs of those around us by doing something concrete. The Letter of Saint James warns us that works are also crucial to Christian discipleship:

> What good is it, my brothers, if someone says he has faith but does not have works? Can that faith save him? If a brother or sister has nothing to wear and has no food for the day, and one of you says to them, "Go in peace, keep warm, and eat well," but you do not give them the necessities of the body, what good is it? So also faith of itself, if it does not have works, is dead. (2:14–17).

By putting his faith into action, Blessed Frédéric Ozanam is a married saint who lived well this passage from Saint James. Today we look at Frédéric's life, words, and works in the hopes that it will inspire us to do more faith-filled works.

Born in France in 1813 in the period following the French Revolution, Frédéric grew up in a time when people were quickly turning their backs on the Church. In this dark period, he did not retreat in despair but instead became a beacon of light proclaiming truth not only in word but also in deed. Frédéric trained first as a lawyer and then eventually became a professor of medieval literature. During his time of intense academic formation, he would gather with friends to hash out the questions of the day. The intellectually stimulating gatherings attracted believers and nonbelievers alike. During one meeting, a student asked Frédéric a question that changed his life: "What is your Church doing now? What is She doing for the poor of Paris? Show us your works and we will believe you!"

Frédéric took this challenge to heart and started a group that visited the poor in Paris slums. Under the patronage of Saint Vincent de Paul, Frédéric and several others set to work helping those most in need. During a deadly cholera outbreak in the city, the group visited and cared for the ill. Giving from his own necessities rather than from his excess, Frédéric once brought his own winter supply of wood to a widow whose husband had died of cholera. Though he easily could have shielded himself from the world's suffering in a successful academic career, Frédéric remained in touch with the uncomfortable realities of poverty:

> Knowledge of the poor and needy is not gained by poring over books or in discussions with politicians, but by visiting the slums where they live, sitting by the bedside

of the dying, feeling the cold they feel and learning from their lips the causes of their woes.[27]

Clearly, Frédéric did not see his work as burdensome or complicated. He simply did small things to improve the lives of others.

Frédéric once summarized his humble approach to the Works of Mercy, "In my life, I want to become better and do a little good." The group Frédéric formed in his university days followed this simple philosophy and soon became known as the Society of Saint Vincent de Paul. Before his death, the organization had spread worldwide. As Catholics, we too are called to support the needy, whether through our local parish or another organization. When the collection basket comes around during Mass, do we thoughtlessly take a bill out of our wallet, plop it in the basket, and call it a day? While giving money to good causes by tithing to the Church is praiseworthy, we also are called to give our time and money in a more planned and purposeful way.

Every second Friday, our family volunteers at the local soup kitchen, serving food and visiting with the people who go to eat. It's one of our favorite days of the month. We also know some families that periodically pool their charitable giving and unite their energies. When they get together to plan their giving, every family brings and promotes different ideas, and the group works to reach a consensus around a targeted need. Then, for the next few months the families unite their financial resources, volunteer time, and prayer around a specific goal. As married couples, God has a plan for how we are called to give more than just our money to those in need. By giving his time, talent, and treasure to serve the poor, Frédéric's life models for us the way we are called to follow Jesus as Christians. May his life set us afire with encouragement and convict us by its radical witness!

## Spiritual Practice

1. Try to recall a time in the past month when you offered to pray for someone. If you can think of an intention you heard, spend some time praying for it now. Whether it is with an Our Father, Hail Mary, or an extemporaneous prayer, honor your word and the person who entrusted you with this intention by praying an extra prayer for the intention.

2. While prayer is the most powerful thing we can do to help those in need, our actions in response to a person's need can often be their answer to prayer. Can you think of something concrete you could do to help a person who has recently asked you for prayer?

3.  Does the Society of Saint Vincent de Paul do any work in the parish you attend? If so, look into getting involved this month. If there is no Saint Vincent de Paul Society in your parish, look for other means of supporting the poor in your area.

## Closing Prayer

God of Love, please increase our charity and help us to will and act for the good of others. Aid us as a family in discerning how we can help the poor. Amen.

# Voice of a Prophet

## Opening Prayer

### The Benedictus

Blessed be the Lord, the God of Israel,
  for he has visited and brought redemption to
      his people.
He has raised up a horn for our salvation
  within the house of David his servant,
even as he promised through the mouth of his holy
    prophets from of old:
  salvation from our enemies and from the hand of
      all who hate us,
to show mercy to our fathers

and to be mindful of his holy covenant
and of the oath he swore to Abraham our father,
    and to grant us that, rescued from the hand of
        enemies,
without fear we might worship him in holiness and
    righteousness
    before him all our days.
And you, child, will be called prophet of the
    Most High,
    for you will go before the Lord to prepare his
        ways,
to give his people knowledge of salvation
    through the forgiveness of their sins,
because of the tender mercy of our God
    by which the daybreak from on high will visit us
to shine on those who sit in darkness and death's
    shadow,
    to guide our feet into the path of peace.

*Luke 1:68–79*


Rooted in salvation history and the Hebrew prophets' announcement of God's special love for the poor, Catholic social teaching articulates the Christian call to serve those most in need. This teaching is also inspired by Jesus who identified himself with "these least ones" (Mt 25:45). Though commitment to the poor was integral to Christianity from the very beginning of its history, the body of Church teaching around this aspect of the faith only developed in the late nineteenth century. The married saint we continue to discuss today, Blessed Frédéric Ozanam, made significant contributions to the development of this thought. Aspects of his personal approach to serving the poor—particularly his prayer life and zeal for growth—can inspire us as we try to live the social teaching of the Church in our own lives.

Frédéric Ozanam lived during the Industrial Revolution and witnessed the vast movement of people from the country to France's great, dirty cities and factories. He observed the suffering people experienced as they struggled to eke out a living in the cities, alienated from the land and their families. He showed a keen understanding of the dynamics creating and contributing to poverty in his writings:

> The question which is agitating the world today is a social one. It is a struggle between those who have nothing and those who have too much. It is a violent clash of opulence and poverty which is shaking the ground under our feet. Our duty as Christians is to throw ourselves between these two camps in order to accomplish by love, what justice alone cannot do.[28]

Frédéric also wrote elsewhere, "Charity is the Samaritan who pours oil on the wounds of the traveler who has been attacked. But it is justice's role to prevent the attacks." Frédéric's prescient words would be echoed more than 150 years later in Pope Benedict XVI's encyclical *Deus Caritas Est* (God is Love), a letter to all the faithful in which the pope explained the importance of the Church's commitment to charity while its members promote justice in the social order.

Amid chaotic social circumstances, Frédéric easily could have shielded himself from others' suffering and focused only on his academic career and writing about poverty. But his conscience urged him not to blind himself to what was happening around him. He had to act. Frédéric's work for the poor never distracted him from his prayer life. Grounded in the Eucharist, Frédéric knew that works rooted in a deep love for Christ were the only thing that what would fundamentally change society. He was known to say, "The best way to economize time is to 'lose' half an hour each day attending Holy Mass." Finding Christ in the Mass, Frédéric then sought Christ in the poor:

> But the poor we see with the eyes of flesh; they are there and we can put finger and hand in their wounds and the scars of the crown of thorns are visible on their foreheads; and at this point incredulity no longer has place and we should fall at their feet and say with the Apostle, *Tu es Dominus et Deus Meus* (you are my Lord

and my God!). You are our masters, and we will be your servants. You are for us the sacred images of the God we do not see, and not knowing how to love him otherwise shall we not love him in your person?[29]

Frédéric's challenging, prophetic view of the poor can also be seen in Pope Francis' emphasis on serving Christ in the prisoner, the immigrant, the refugee, and in the Catholic no longer sharing in the sacramental life of the Church.

Frédéric's Christian discipleship also inspires in his zeal for continual growth. Never satisfied with the level of his spiritual development or his many works of mercy, Frédéric would say, "Charity must never look to the past, but always to the future, because the number of its past works is still very small and the present and future miseries that it must alleviate are infinite." These words reveal Frédéric's faith-filled hope for what God would do through him in the future. Confident in God's forgiveness of his failings in the past and committed to live for God's glory in the present, Frédéric tried to do just a little more every day for God and neighbor.

Blessed Frédéric's Ozanam's deep prayer life and zeal for continual conversion can inspire and motivate us in our own lives to seek God in all things. Of course, it's important to keep in mind that every married couple experiences shifts in their ability to participate in the

Spiritual and Corporal Works of Mercy. Early in our marriage, with fewer children in tow, social activism was more possible. We worked in youth ministry for a poor, inner-city church and participated in other services to the poor in urban areas. But getting out to visit the homeless became more difficult as our family grew. Now that we have older children, we again have been able to reach out to the poor in concrete ways. Regardless of the season of your family's life, the power to serve those in need (whether through praying novenas or serving food to the homeless) comes from something that is always available—a close connection with Christ who lives in the poor. Time spent in mental prayer, in reading God's Word, and in the presence of the Blessed Sacrament helps us to see Christ in the poor and to desire to love him there.

## Spiritual Practice

1. Do you prefer doing charitable work, working in the social order for justice, or both? Why do you feel that way? As a couple how do you choose to help in your neighborhood, at home, and at work?

2. How often do you go to daily Mass? Consider taking Frédéric's advice to "lose" a half hour by going to daily Mass sometime this week.

3. Does your parish have groups dedicated to the Works of Mercy? Are there any nearby ecumenical groups doing Works of Mercy? Consider looking for a project to get involved in. If there aren't any available opportunities, think about starting something in your parish.

## Closing Prayer

Father of Mercy, give us the grace to see Christ in the poor and fill our hearts with charity so that we might be a Good Samaritan to those in need. Amen.

# DAY 21

---

# Marriage for the Other

## Opening Prayer

Lord, let our hearts be set aflame with love for one an-other. May we love each other more than life, because this passing life is nothing. And may our only hope be that we pass through this life in such a way that in the world to come we will be united in perfect love with God himself.

*Inspired by Saint John Chrysostom's Homily 20,*
*on Ephesians 5*

Blessed Frédéric Ozanam was a man who loved not only in word but also in deed, often saying, "I am weary of words—let us act!" He lived this out not only in his work for the poor but also in his personal life, especially in his marriage. As a young man, Frédéric carefully discerned a call to married life and earnestly worked to be spiritually worthy of his spouse, approaching his marriage as he did all his endeavors—as a means to perfection in charity. Today we will look at how Frédéric's humility, tenderness, and devotion to his wife, Amélie, can be a model and an inspiration for all married couples.

Before his marriage, Frédéric wrote to a friend describing the qualities he hoped to find in his future wife:

> I pray that she may present herself as late as possible, when I will have become worthy of her. . . . above all I pray that she will be endowed with an exceptional soul, with great virtues; that she may be infinitely better than I am; that she may lead me upward and never let me descend; that she may be courageous, since I am so often pusillanimous; that she may be fervent for the faith, since I am so often lukewarm in the things of God.[30]

Humble words from the man who just two years earlier had founded the Society of Saint Vincent de Paul! In time, Frédéric found the devoted partner in charity he had sought, Amélie Soulacroix. The first time he saw Amélie, she was caring for her disabled brother. (After their marriage, the couple would take Amélie's brother into their home.) The instant Frédéric saw his future wife compassionately caring for her brother, his heart brimmed with love.

Frédéric thought himself unworthy of his wife and loved her tenderly. The gratitude and tenderness he felt for his wife is evident in his letters. In a letter he penned to a friend describing his wedding Mass he wrote, "Last Wednesday at ten o'clock in the morning, in the church of Saint Nizier, your friend was on his knees . . . At his side you would have seen a veiled young girl dressed in white, pious as an angel, and already—she gives me leave to say it—tender and affectionate as a friend."[31] He later described the incredible joy he felt to be with Amélie on their honeymoon: "I do not count days or hours. Time does not exist for me. . . . Happiness in the present is eternity. I understand what heaven means. Help me to be good and grateful."[32]

Though not without difficulty, Amélie and Frédéric's marriage was full of happiness because they worked to keep their love for one another alive. Over the years, Frédéric continued to show love for his wife by regularly celebrating their marriage anniversary. On the twenty-third of every month, the date of their wedding, he would present Amélie with a bouquet of flowers. Simple, loving gestures like these helped to create a firmer foundation for Amélie and Frédéric's marriage. They also regularly praised and encouraged one another, which strengthened their relationship. For instance, Frédéric once wrote to Amélie, "Your faith will indeed sustain mine. . . . When doubts assail me, when difficulties trouble my conscience, when fears for the future terrify me, I shall grow calm in thinking of you."[33]

Amélie and Frédéric's loving relationship shows how couples are better able to rise to challenges when they feel supported and loved. Small acts of love for our spouse can accumulate and become emotional resources that he or she can draw on in times of difficulty. When we feel needed, important, and worthy in the eyes of our spouse, we are more apt to respond well when our marriages are under strain. We can build up our spouses' resources in very simple ways—with a few more smiles than usual; a quick touch on the shoulder; a "thank you" for a mundane task typically taken for granted (laundry, garbage duty, etc.); an extra-long kiss hello or goodbye; or a silly note on the bathroom mirror. We may not be around the next time dinner is burning in the oven and a child has wet the bed. Or when work goes badly, and the car battery dies in the parking lot. But in these moments, our spouses can remember our words of affection and encouragement and feel consoled. We respond more gracefully to life's difficulties when we know we are deeply loved by our spouses, and we have the memories of loving actions to prove it.

Amélie and Frédéric also model for us a marriage that did not wait for the other spouse to act before showing love. Married couples can easily fall into the habit of not showing love for one another when we are waiting for the other person to act first. We might think, "Well, I would do more X" (insert something your spouse would like you to do), "if only my spouse would start doing more Y" (insert something you want your spouse to do more). Catholic psychologist and marriage expert Gregory Popcak calls this "marital chicken." Most married couples can relate to this dynamic. But when spouses make it a habit to wait for the other person to show love before budging an inch themselves, it's a happiness destroyer. Small gestures, like the bouquet of flowers Frédéric would offer his wife every month, can make a more positive impact on our marriages than we might realize. Certainly, it takes prayer and work, but we too can follow in their footsteps. Like Frédéric, let us implore God to make us worthy of our spousal vocation. In our marriages, may we act as partners on the journey to Christ, always making love our aim.

*Blessed Frédéric Ozanam, pray for us!*

# Spiritual Practice

1. Do you remember your wedding anniversary yearly? What about your "monthiversary"? Resolve to do something special for your spouse this month. Be precise about what you plan to do, since precision increases the likelihood of remembering and following through.

2. Do you ever find yourself saying, "I'd do more romantic things if I felt more romantic? But I don't want to be fake!" Love is in the will. The best way to show love is to *do* loving things. Then, often, feeling will begin to follow action. Choose one way to show love for your spouse tomorrow, even if you don't feel like it (perhaps especially if you don't feel like it!).

3. Discuss the concept of "marital chicken" with your spouse and find some examples in your marriage. Consider some ways that you can work toward reducing this dynamic in your relationship.

# Closing Prayer

Lord, we pray for the courage to love one another with the gift of our whole selves while striving to bring one another to heaven. Amen.

# Saint Monica

*c. 331–387*

# DAY 22

---

# A Steadfast Support

## Opening Prayer

Heavenly Father, inspire us to have an intense and true love for our spouse that is willing to move the heavens for his or her sake. Help us to remember always that "Love is patient; love is kind; love is not envious or boastful or arrogant or rude. It does not insist on its own way; it is not irritable or resentful; it does not rejoice in wrongdoing, but rejoices in the truth. It bears all things, believes all things, hopes all things, endures all things" (1 Cor 13:4–7, NRSV). Pour forth, oh Lord, we pray, this love into our hearts!

Today we travel several centuries back in time from Blessed Frédéric Ozanam in the nineteenth century to Saint Monica in the fourth century. Monica is perhaps best-known as the mother of her wayward son, Augustine, who had a momentous conversion and went to become a saint and a Doctor of the Church (we will talk more about him tomorrow). Today we'll examine Monica's witness that teaches us how to steadfastly support our spouse in the journey of faith, even when a couple's steps aren't exactly in sync.

Monica was born around the year 331 in Thagaste, Africa. Among the first generation of Christian Africans, her parents arranged a marriage for Monica with an older pagan man, Patricius. Why they chose a pagan spouse for Monica remains a mystery. Thankfully, Patricius was tolerant of Christianity. Unfortunately, while at times Patricius was good-natured and loving to his wife and family, at other times he was violent and had a terrible temper. In a time when women with abusive husbands had few options, Monica was faced with what must have seemed like a hopeless situation. She had an arranged marriage to a man who was violent, faithless, and engaged in numerous infidelities. But she did not lose hope and instead chose to put her trust in God. Though her husband criticized her faith, Monica ignored his disdain and dedicated her time to prayer and charity, giving to the poor and serving those in need. Through her prayer, patience, and virtuous example, the Holy Spirit worked to influence Patricius over time and eventually produced a miraculous outcome. To Monica's great joy, after twenty years of marriage, Patricius was baptized shortly before his death.

If you're reading this couples' devotional with your spouse, you might find it difficult to relate to Monica's experience. Perhaps you are blessed to have a spouse who is supportive of your faith, and you both pursue the common goal of heaven together. Or maybe you can relate to Monica and are reading this devotional by yourself or with a highly reluctant spouse. Either way, at some point we all are guilty of neglecting to support our spouse and to prioritize his or her spiritual wellbeing. Even two believing spouses will disagree with one another about issues of the faith, often in just simple ways. For instance, imagine you have just finished Saint Teresa of Ávila's *Interior Castle.* You're over the moon about the book and think it will be *exactly* what your husband needs. Thirty pages in, he can't make heads or tails of it and is completely disinterested. You're left feeling irritated and a bit angry. Sometimes unfair expectations that our spouse always will be on the same "spiritual page" can lead to feelings of loneliness, being misunderstood, frustration, and bitterness—that can set couples up for disaster.

Different spiritual tools help people at different times in life. When we find something helpful that our spouse does not, instead of despairing, we can pray that he or she will receive the same spiritual fruit we have received in whatever form the Holy Spirit wishes to give it.

Another challenge for married couples can occur when spouses experience the faith differently from one another and have differing opinions or approaches. For instance, perhaps your spouse is making great strides in his or her spiritual life and experiencing consolation and peace. This can be difficult when we ourselves are feeling like we're walking through a spiritual Sahara Desert, far from God and his peace. Couples can support one another by being sensitive to how each person is experiencing the spiritual journey, resisting smugness or bitterness, and simply praying for and with our spouse instead. At the same time, patience has its rewards so couples should also look for and provide for times when they can rejoice together in shared consolation. For example, a couple may feel the closeness of God during the baptism of a new child, when reading Scripture together, or when praying together before the Eucharist. In these situations, we can rejoice together—just as Monica and Patricius must have rejoiced at the moment of his baptism. May Saint Monica's example of tireless prayer, support, and charity for her husband give us the eyes to see the many ways we each can better pray for and encourage our spouse, as we walk together with Christ.

## Spiritual Practice

1. Are there big or small areas in your life where you would like more support from your spouse? Think and pray about it, and if the Holy Spirit is leading you to do so, discuss these areas with your spouse in an atmosphere of generosity, charity, and assumed good will.

2. Is there one specific area in which you feel you could support your spouse better? Resolve to do so! And if you are inspired, tell your spouse of your resolution.

3. Have there been times in your marriage when your spouse was experiencing consolation and growth in the spiritual life and you were not, or vice versa? How did you handle that situation? Discuss with your spouse how you experienced times such as these.

## Closing Prayer

God, our rock and mighty fortress, grant that we may be pillars of strength and encouragement for one other in the highs and lows of marriage. Though our spiritual journeys may sometimes take different paths, may we never lose sight of our love for one another and our heavenly destination. Amen.

# DAY 23

## Praying for Loved Ones

### Opening Prayer

*If you do not have children, pray for your godchildren, nieces, nephews, future children, or anyone to whom you have been a spiritual parent.*

O Heavenly Father, we commend to you any children who are entrusted to our care. Be their God and Father and mercifully supply whatever is wanting in us, through frailty or negligence. Strengthen all children to overcome the corruptions of the world, to resist all solicitations to evil, whether from within or without. Deliver them from the secret snares of the enemy and pour your grace into their hearts. Confirm and multiply in them the gifts of the Holy Spirit that daily they may grow in grace and in the knowledge of our Lord Jesus Christ. Faithfully serving you here, may we come to rejoice in your presence in heaven. Amen.

When her husband passed away, Monica was left alone to raise their three children—Augustine, Navigius, and Perpetua. Her eldest, Augustine, was seventeen when his father died. While Monica's faith and holiness seemed to have a good influence on Navigius and Perpetua, Augustine ignored his mother's pleas to put God first. Instead, he was only interested in success and pleasure. Like many parents today who worry when their children abandon the faith, Monica was concerned for her son's salvation. As she watched Augustine fall further and further away from Christ, she prayed fervently for him. Monica's example can strengthen us in our steadfast prayer for our spouse, for our children (if we have them), and for any friends and family who have abandoned the sacraments.

Perhaps no other moment was as heart-wrenching for Monica as the time when Augustine returned from Carthage to his hometown to teach. What should have been a happy homecoming was instead a bitter disappointment. Augustine was unmarried yet had fathered a son with a woman he was unable to marry because of social standing. Her son also had joined a heretical sect, the Manicheans. Monica found it all unbearable. Weary of heart, she refused at first to allow her son into her home, and she stormed heaven in continual prayer. In his mercy, God sent Monica a consoling dream in which she saw herself with Augustine in the presence of Christ. Comforted by her dream, Monica welcomed her wayward son, his common-law wife, and her grandson into her home. She must have hoped that by her physical proximity and example she could influence her son to become Christian.

For years, Monica continued to pray constantly for her eldest son's conversion. In his autobiography *Confessions*, Augustine would later describe his mother's unceasing prayers:

> My mother, Your faithful one, wept to You for me, more than mothers weep the bodily deaths of their children. For she, by that faith and spirit which she had from You, discerned that I lay in death, and you heard her, O Lord; You heard her, and despised not her tears when streaming down, they watered the ground under her eyes in every place where she prayed.[34]

Augustine also wrote that his mother was "zealous in her weeping and mourning"[35] as she unceasingly prayed for her son. He recalled, "O my God, in the secret purpose of Your providence, you did not forsake my soul; and out of the blood of my mother's heart, through her tears night and day poured out, she was a sacrifice offered for me unto God."[36] Though it must have felt like Augustine was immune to his mother's pain and prayers, he clearly was observing and took to heart, to at least some extent, her desire for him to convert.

After some time living with Monica in his hometown in Africa, Augustine then made plans to move to Milan to further his career. Intending to leave his mother behind, he lied to his mother about what time the ship was set to sail. But Monica would not be deterred. When she realized her son had left, she set sail on another boat and tracked Augustine down in Milan. There she continued her vigil of tears. This time, she found a partner in prayer—the master rhetorician and bishop, Saint Ambrose. Ambrose's advice to Monica and his eventual discussions with Augustine would be instrumental in her son's acceptance of the faith. Monica's prayers had led her son precisely to the kind of learned, holy man who could help him. Later, when he began to make steps toward the faith, Augustine wrote that his mother "loved [Ambrose] as an angel of God, because she knew that by him I had been brought for the present to that doubtful state of faith I now was in."[37]

Unfortunately, it's often most difficult to share the Gospel with those who are closest to us. And at times it's our own faults that veil the goodness of Christ and our unlearned speech that makes his truth less clear. While we always are called to witness to the Gospel, we might find that some of our loved ones are not open to hearing about Jesus. This can be particularly difficult when our own children turn away from the faith and choose to ignore the beautiful truth that we have been saved by Jesus Christ. In these situations, parents naturally desire their children's happiness in the faith and fear for their salvation. When we despair of our loved ones' salvation, we can turn to prayer as Monica did and trust in God's goodness and power. As much as we want our loved ones to get to heaven, God wants it more! And while our example and words are significant, our prayers to the Father are even more important. Let us turn then to Monica's intercession for our loved ones and never cease in prayer for their conversion!

## Spiritual Practice

1. When was the last time you invited someone into closer relationship with Christ? Say a prayer for the courage to do this more often and for the prudence to be led by the Holy Spirit to find the right moment and words.

2. Bring to mind the children in your life, whether biological or adopted, godchildren, or any other

spiritual children. How often do you pray for them? In this next week, consider praying a Rosary or an Our Father for each child you brought to mind.

3. Is there anyone who could join you in your efforts to help the children in your life? Are there other members of your church community who might be willing to join you in prayer for them? Any canonized saints whose intercession you might want to seek? Maybe Saint Ambrose, Saint Augustine, or Saint Monica?

## Closing Prayer

God, please give us a heart that breaks for those who are outside the Church, especially for those family members closest to us. Give us the strength to pray and sacrifice for their conversion and to be a good example to them. We especially pray for the children in our lives, that they may know you and that we may rejoice with them eternally in heaven. Amen.

# The Beauty of Truth

## Opening Prayer

### Prayer to Our God of Truth

O God of truth, grant me the happiness of heaven so that, according to your promise, my joy may be full. Until then, let my mind dwell on that happiness; my tongue speak of it, my heart long for it, my mouth proclaim it, my soul hunger for it, my flesh thirst for it, and my entire being desire it until I enter through death into the joy of my Lord forever. Amen.

*Saint Augustine*

After his conversion, Augustine wrote of his mother, Monica, "I can find no words to express how intensely she loved me: with far more anxious solicitude did she give birth to me in the spirit than ever she had in the flesh."[38] Much as a mother suffers through pain and tears to bring her child into the world, Monica tearfully toiled and suffered to bring Augustine to Jesus. Thankfully, her labors were not in vain. In time God turned Monica's bitter weeping to tears of joy. Her son Augustine not only would be baptized, but he also would become a holy bishop, a canonized saint, and a revered Doctor of the Church. Today we will examine how God responded to Monica's prayers with an abundance of grace and turned a story of a mother's sorrow into a beautiful tale of conversion to the truth.

When Augustine was in Milan, though he was not yet able to bring himself to live the virtue of chastity, he slowly began to see the truth of Christianity. Desiring to convert but still in a state of anguish and confusion, he was walking in a garden one day when he heard the voice of a child say, "Take up and read; take up and read."[39] He ran nearby to the place where he had left a volume of Saint Paul's letters. He opened to a page at random and read, "Not in orgies and drunkenness, not in promiscuity and licentiousness, not in rivalry and jealousy. But put on the Lord Jesus Christ, and make no provision for the desires of the flesh" (Rom 13:13–14). In these words were the answers to Monica's prayers. The grace of God triumphed in that moment and Augustine began to change his life to conform to the truth. Knowing the role his mother's prayers played in his search for the truth, Augustine immediately shared the news of his conversion with Monica. Together they rejoiced and praised the Lord.

Augustine would later pray, thanking God for answering Monica's prayers, "You turned her grief into a gladness, much more plentiful than she had desired."[40] Finally united together in the Body of Christ, Augustine relates how, after his conversion, mother and son were both given a beautiful visionary experience:

> She and I stood alone, leaning in a certain window, which looked into the garden of the house where we occupied at Ostia. Removed from the crowd, we were recovering from the fatigues of a long journey. . . . We were discoursing then together, alone, very pleasantly; and forgetting those things which are behind and reaching forth unto those things which are before we were enquiring between ourselves in the presence of the Truth, which You are, of what sort the eternal life of the saints was to be.[41]

As they gazed out a window upon a garden, it's as if God gave them a glimpse that was at once back into Eden and forward into the beatific vision of God. While they were talking, Monica said to Augustine, "Son, for my part I do not delight anymore in anything in this life. What I do here any longer, and to what end I am here, I know not, now that my hopes in this world are accomplished. One thing I desired was to linger for a while in this life, that I might see you become a Catholic Christian before I died. My God has done this for me more abundantly."[42] Shortly after this holy conversation in which mother and son rejoiced in the truth, Monica died.

Monica and Augustine's conversation began in admiration of the beauty of this world and worked its way into the realm of heavenly realities until they could no longer speak at all. We may not be granted the grace of a mystical conversation like the one they had. But we can catch a glimpse of heaven by looking for and appreciating the beauty and truth that God places in our everyday lives. Maybe it's just the way your spouse smiles just so in response to a witty remark. Or how your baby son scrunches up his nose when you try to feed him a new food. The pink twilight that your young daughter points out to you from her window as you tuck her in. Or a spiritual book that helps you to raise your mind to God's truth. Or an excellent homily at Mass. All these seemingly mundane experiences are really opportunities to appreciate the beauty and truth in our everyday lives. If we learn to appreciate these things on earth, we will be readier to appreciate them when we meet he who is Truth and Beauty itself—God. May Saint Monica, who led her son Augustine to the Truth with her prayers, also lead us to Jesus with her prayers.

*Saint Monica, pray for us!*

## Spiritual Practice

1. How often do you stop to appreciate beauty and truth in your everyday life? Together with your spouse, spend some time listing those things in your life that show you glimpses of heaven. Then thank God for them!

2. Have you and your spouse ever been led to wonder and awe through God's creation? Spend some time together remembering the experience.

3. Make concrete plans to enjoy God's creation sometime in the next month, even if it's just by taking a walk.

## Closing Prayer

Heavenly Father, we pray for the grace to become like a stained-glass window through which God's grandeur can stream. Help us to rise above the things of this world and to rest in your love that transcends all things. May we stop and appreciate the glimpses of heaven you give to us each day. Amen.

# Saints Basil the Elder and Emmelia

*c. 270 – c. 349 (Basil)*
*Died c. 372 (Emmelia)*

# Forming a Holy Family

## Opening Prayer

### Prayer to the Eucharistic Jesus

Dear Jesus, in the sacrament of the altar, may you be forever thanked and praised. Love, worthy of all celestial and earthly love! Love, who out of infinite love for us, ungrateful sinners, did assume our human nature, shed your most precious Blood in the cruel scourging, and expired on a shameful Cross for our eternal salvation! Now illumined with lively faith, with the outpouring of our whole souls and the fervor of our hearts, we humbly beseech you, through the infinite merits of your painful sufferings, give us strength and courage to destroy every evil passion that sways our hearts, to bless you by the exact fulfillment of our duties, to supremely to hate all sin, and to support one another in becoming saints. Amen.[43]

Today we are going to look at a family that, in many ways, resembled the model for all human families, the Holy Family. Saints Basil and Emmelia were a married couple from the fourth century who lived in what is now modern-day Turkey. Basil came from a saintly family. His mother, Saint Macrina the Elder, was educated in the Christian faith by the holy bishop, Saint Gregory Thaumaturgus. Tried in the fire of the Diocletian persecutions, Macrina's family fled into the forest for seven years to hunt and forage until the persecutions ended. Basil was thus reared in a family that understood and lived out the sufferings of Christ in a real way. Emmelia's family faced similar struggles. Orphaned at an early age, she was the daughter of a martyr for the faith. Formed by this powerful legacy of holiness, Basil and Emmelia would go on to raise children who would prove powerfully capable of leading others to Christ.

Known for their works of charity, Basil and Emmelia did a great deal for the impoverished. The main evidence of their holiness lay in how they raised their children. Basil and Emmelia had ten children and, astoundingly, six became saints. Their children include Saint Basil the

Great and Saint Gregory of Nyssa, both bishops and Fathers of the Church; Saint Naucratius; Saint Macrina the Younger; Saint Theosebia, a virgin and deaconess; and the youngest, Saint Peter of Sebaste, who became a bishop and helped his mother and sister Macrina the Younger establish a monastic community. Basil and Emmelia were so successful in their parenting that their own children soon surpassed them in holy wisdom. When Naucratius died at age twenty-seven, Emmelia was heartbroken until Macrina, her wise, eldest daughter, reminded her that Christians must not mourn as if they had no hope. This was not the only time that Macrina spurred her family on to holiness. Many of Macrina's siblings followed her example by making a vow of chastity. Also, with Macrina's encouragement, Emmelia began a community of nuns after her husband's death.

Basil and Emmelia raised such saintly children by influencing their children in three areas: (1) they took special care in educating their children in Scripture; (2) they taught their children to pray; (3) they invited their children to consider a call to religious or priestly life. We too can influence the children in our lives, whether our own or others entrusted to our physical or spiritual care, by following Emmelia and Basil's example.

First, we can strive to prioritize the Christian education of our children. Parents and godparents can easily be tempted to outsource children's religious education, entrusting it strictly to "professionals." But parents are the first and most competent teachers of their children. In *Familiaris Consortio*, Saint John Paul II calls the family a "school of following Christ" (no. 39) and a "school of deeper humanity" (no. 21). Putting Christ at the center, not simply for one hour a week but all the time, can make a real difference in children's lives. Teaching children the faith does not mean that we must be experts. Children often ask puzzling questions like, "The Bible says God hardened Pharaoh's heart. If God hardened his heart, how can Pharaoh's choices be considered evil?" When they ask difficult questions, we don't have to punt them. Instead, we can embrace the opportunity to humbly seek the truth together.

Second, following in the example of Basil and Emmelia, we can teach our children to pray. Acting like seasoned "prayer experts" will not help children learn to pray as much as modeling a prayer life that grows and develops. We can also model a variety of different ways to pray (spontaneous and written, hymns, etc.) while also setting up a solid routine of prayer throughout the day. We also shouldn't be afraid to allow our children, even the young ones, to lead family prayer. Our two-year-old is sometimes the best at thank-you-God prayers. When we teach our children to pray at all times—in stress, trouble, and joy, we teach them resilience because they learn to rely on God always. After a fall and a scrape or even just a close call, we can pray the *Guardian Angel Prayer* with our children, to remind them of the spiritual protection that always surrounds them.

Finally, we can imitate Emmelia and Basil's willingness to invite those around us to consider the religious life or the priesthood. If we don't tell children entrusted to our care that they might have a call to the religious or priestly life, who will? Emmelia and Basil's family of saints is truly amazing, but, with God's help, we too can turn our families over to God to form them into saints. Emmelia and Basil's family is evidence that holiness catches, and, under the right conditions, spreads like wildfire. While our families may not face the same trials of severe persecutions and martyrdom, we can still strive to instill in our children the same steadfast faith and unshakable trust in the Lord. May we, too, be part of a legacy of saints!

*Saints Emmelia and Basil the Elder, pray for us!*

## Spiritual Practice

1. What are your family's favorite ways to pray? Have you ever considered reading a very short passage

from Scripture each day with your spouse or children? If you don't already, commit to beginning some kind of consistent prayer with your family.

2. Do you own a *Catechism of the Catholic Church*? This is a great resource to look for answers to the tough questions. If you don't own one, you can find it online. Choose a passage to read together today.

3. Have you ever talked about the priesthood or religious life with the children in your life? If not, look for an opportunity to bring up the topic.

## Closing Prayer

Father, Son, and Holy Spirit, increase our faith! Help us to understand the Blessed Trinity and unite us to your life and love. May our faith remain strong, withstand all trial, and spread like wildfire to those around us. Give us the courage and grace to attend to the faith life of the children entrusted to our care and help us to encourage them to listen to God's will for their life. Amen.

# The Power of Friendship in Christ

## Opening Prayer

### A Prayer for Our Friends

Jesus, as you brought light to this dark world, you often had supportive and loving friends around you. Help us always to be good friends to one another in our marriage so that we may encourage one another in holiness. Please also help us to find and maintain other good friendships that focus on bringing your love and light to the world. As the Apostle Paul prayed for his friends in his first letter to the Colossians, we also pray that our friends may be "filled with the knowledge of his will through all spiritual wisdom and understanding to live in a manner worthy of the Lord, so as to be fully pleasing, in every good work bearing fruit and growing in the knowledge of God, strengthened with every power, in accord with his glorious might, for all endurance and patience, with joy giving thanks to the Father" (Col 1:9–12). Amen.

Many married couples consider themselves to be best friends. But what exactly does friendship with our spouse and with others entail? What kind of friendships do we hope our children will develop? How should we look at friendship in terms of our life in Christ? Today we answer some of these questions by returning to the inspiring family of Saints Emmelia and Basil the Elder. Yesterday, we discussed how the seeds of their family's holiness were watered by attentiveness to religious education, prayer together, and encouragement to follow God's call. This family, however, had another, powerful, secret weapon that helped them on their path to heaven: friendship. Today we will examine the friendship between Emmelia and Basil's son, Saint Basil the Great, and Saint Gregory of Nazianzus. While the consideration of married saints may seem to exclude discussing the friendship of two celibate bishops, their relationship reveals how important true friendship is for all holy vocations.

Aristotle wrote about three kinds of friendships, distinguishing them from one other by the good pursued: (1) friendships of pleasure, where pleasurable goods (e.g., sports, stamp-collecting) are pursued together; friendships of utility (e.g., friends at work) where useful goods are pursued together; and friendships of virtue or character (e.g., hopefully your spouse or friends at Church), where virtue is pursued together. Most people enjoy all these different types of friendship, but the last is the most precious. The Book of Sirach (Ben Sira) describes this third kind of friendship well:

> Faithful friends are a sturdy shelter;
>> whoever finds one finds a treasure.
> Faithful friends are beyond price,
>> no amount can balance their worth.
> Faithful friends are life-saving medicine;
>> those who fear God will find them (6:14–16).

Aristotle was not Christian, but he hit on the very important truth that friendship can lead us toward the good. As Christians, we know that the ultimate good is God. True friends, in other words, are more than just pals who accompany us as we hang out at a club or go to the movies. Rather, true friends help us to live for heaven.

Gregory of Nazianzus describes this kind of friendship in his funeral oration for his best friend, Saint Basil the Great:

The sole business of both of us was virtue, and living for the hopes to come . . . With a view to this, all our life and actions were directed . . . we sharpened upon each other our weapons of virtue . . . we were a rule and standard to each other, for the distinction between what was right and what was not.[44]

The two friends spurred one another along the path to holiness and everlasting life. Gregory of Nazianzus further wrote, "In my opinion, nothing is of value, save that which leads to virtue and to the improvement of its devotees. Different men have different names, derived from their fathers, their families, their pursuits, their exploits: we had but one great business and name—to be and to be called Christians."[45] The heaven-focused friendship of Gregory of Nazianzus and Basil the Great models the joys of true friendship and a shared life in Christ.

Saints Gregory of Nazianzus and Basil the Great's holy friendship shows us that true friends share in our faith, spur us on to greater holiness, and are models of Christian discipleship. Hopefully, we have already found such a friend in our spouse. For that we should be eternally grateful. Even if we are blessed with a spouse who shares our faith and focuses on heaven, other friendships outside of marriage can also support our efforts toward holiness. Faithful friends can strengthen a marriage, as both spouses learn from and are encouraged by their friendships. The growth a spouse experiences in friendship spills over into his or her marriage and family life, that then helps the entire Christian community to grow in holiness. For married couples who have children, modeling good and holy friendships is particularly important because it helps children to then choose friends wisely and to be good friends to others. Living the joy of friendships focused on Christ can help us on our journey to heaven. With the grace of God, may we endeavor to develop not only a holy friendship with our spouse but with others who will help us to grow in holiness!

Saints Gregory of Nazianzus and Basil the Great, pray for us!

## Spiritual Practice

1. Consider your relationship with your spouse. Do you consider him or her a friend? Do you help one another to grow in virtue? How? Are you models of Christian discipleship for one another? How could you improve your friendship to ensure a solid foundation as you both strive together for eternal life?

2. Consider your other friendships. Do each of you have various kinds of friendships? Does one of

you have more supportive, faithful friends than the other? Discuss your various friendships with your spouse and describe to one another how these friendships help or hinder your faith journey.

3. Do you have one friendship that could grow to be more focused on Christ? Write down a few concrete things you could do to improve the quality of your friendships.

## Closing Prayer

Lord, thank you for all the friendships in our lives. Please help us to be better friends to one another and to others. May our friendships always be rooted in Christ and nourish our marriage, our family, and the wider Christian community. Amen.

# Saints Louis and Zélie Martin

*August 22, 1823–July 29, 1894 (Louis)*
*December 23, 1831–August 28, 1877 (Zélie)*

# An Unchosen Adventure

## Opening Prayer

### Psalm 139:1–18

Lord, you have probed me, you know me:
　　you know when I sit and stand;
　　you understand my thoughts from afar.
You sift through my travels and my rest;
　　with all my ways you are familiar.
Even before a word is on my tongue,
　　Lord, you know it all.
Behind and before you encircle me
　　and rest your hand upon me.
Such knowledge is too wonderful for me,
　　far too lofty for me to reach.

Where can I go from your spirit?

From your presence, where can I flee?

If I ascend to the heavens, you are there;

if I lie down in Sheol, there you are.

If I take the wings of dawn

and dwell beyond the sea,

Even there your hand guides me,

your right hand holds me fast.

If I say, "Surely darkness shall hide me,

and night shall be my light"—

Darkness is not dark for you,

and night shines as the day.

Darkness and light are but one.

You formed my inmost being;

you knit me in my mother's womb.

I praise you, because I am wonderfully made;

wonderful are your works!

My very self you know.

My bones are not hidden from you,

When I was being made in secret,

fashioned in the depths of the earth.

Your eyes saw me unformed;

in your book all are written down;

my days were shaped, before one came to be.

How precious to me are your designs, O God;

how vast the sum of them!

Were I to count them, they would outnumber
   the sands;
   when I complete them, still you are with me.

You already may be familiar with Saints Louis and Zélie Martin, who are known to many as the parents of Saint Thérèse of Lisieux. While their holy parenting of Thérèse was remarkable, this couple is remarkable in many ways. Louis and Zélie had nine children together; four died as infants, and five entered religious life. Such joyful fruitfulness is a bit surprising considering that before marrying, both Zélie and Louis had hoped to pursue religious vocations. Though they both greatly desired to dedicate themselves to the religious life, they also were sensitive to God's voice in their lives and followed where he led. Today we will examine how this inspiring couple allowed God to guide them away from their initial plans to correspond to his mysterious will that would eventually touch so many people.

Zélie Guérin was born on December 23, 1831. Her older sister, Marie, became a cloistered Visitation nun. The two sisters were very close and maintained a lively correspondence. Zélie admired her sister Marie's vocation and hoped to follow in her footsteps and enter religious life. With this intention, Zélie went for an interview with the superior of the Daughters of Charity in Alençon.

During the interview, the superior insisted that it was not God's will that Zélie enter. She left despondent. Like Zélie, Louis Martin also fell in love with religious life and wanted to dedicate himself completely to God. The quiet beauty and the serene prayer of the monastic life called to him so he tried to join the monastery of Grand-Saint-Bernard in Switzerland. Louis' inability to learn Latin cut short his dream. Though initially bitterly disappointed that they could not enter religious life, Louis and Zélie nevertheless continued to pray for guidance.

What must have seemed like a setback for Zélie and Louis was actually a step forward in God's plan. They both were being trained in an invaluable skill—how to listen to God's will. While still reeling from her rejection from the convent, Zélie heard an interior voice from God, "Learn Point d'Alencon." Zélie immediately went to a professional school to learn this fine, rare form of lace-making that requires painstaking patience, intricate precision, and exceptional skill. After some time, Zélie became well-known for her skill and ran her own lace-making business. Around the same time, Louis Martin fell in love with the intricate, careful art of watchmaking. The tiny gears, the precise timing, and the attention to detail all spoke to his meticulous character. Slowly, like the ticking hands of a clock, God was leading Louis and Zélie away from their own plans and toward his own.

Although neither Louis nor Zélie were particularly drawn to the vocation of marriage, the elements began to fall into place for their future together. Louis' mother met Zélie at a lacemaking class, where she immediately recognized in the young woman the wife of her prayers—and hopefully her son's dreams. She arranged for Zélie to meet Louis. But, providentially, one day before the introduction, Zélie happened to be crossing the Bridge of Saint Léonard when she passed a young man who caught her attention. As Zélie looked at the man, she heard an interior voice from God saying, "This is he whom I have prepared for you." The man was Louis Martin. Upon meeting the next day, Louis and Zélie quickly recognized and accepted that God's plan for them was marriage. They also both, however, desired to remain celibate. They preferred to keep their marriage like that of Mary and Joseph: a sharing of life but not of sexual intimacy. With the help of a wise priest and prayer, Louis and Zélie soon realized, that God's will was otherwise. The priest explained to them that because marriage is ordered toward procreation, it involves a call to be open to children.

Louis and Zélie's openness to the truth of the priest's advice is a clear example of how the couple listened to the will of God and adjusted their wills to be more in line with his plan rather than their own. In marriage, it's important to imitate this great couple in the way they tried to listen to God in the little and the big things. Sometimes, it's difficult to follow God's will even in what seem like rather mundane decisions. For instance, our family has moved several times, between cities and within the same city. We prefer spacious, Victorian-style homes. We want to be open to filling the home with children and to radical hospitality, whether by hosting events or welcoming those in need for a period of time. We also love that architectural style and would really prefer it. Despite our best laid plans, God often chooses homes for us that we would not have chosen for ourselves. But each home has also served exactly the purpose God had for us. Once we bought a rather ugly looking home with a cinder-block exterior. But the house also had a living room large enough to host groups of college students for weekly discussions about faith. Our current home is a ranch house built in the sixties, a style neither of us likes. But the large kitchen opens up onto the living room and several nearby bedrooms, enabling us to host large groups in the evening while caring for our children. All our homes, no matter how small, have come with adequate space to continue what we feel is a call to hospitality in our marriage. So, while we still wish that God would provide us with a gabled-roof Victorian home with bay windows, we strive now to just be thankful for the wonderful homes he has provided.

The lives of Louis and Zélie lives show us that the almighty, ever-living God, whose providence and omniscience spans all times and seasons, will often choose adventures for us that we would not have chosen ourselves. Though we may think we know better than God how to do good, if it's not the good to which God has called us, we can be sure it will not lead us to our greatest happiness. Ultimately, the most important thing in marriage is not the perfect home (or the perfect car or job, etc.). Rather, it's to do what Louis and Zélie did—listen to God's will and follow it, even if it's not exactly what we prefer! Zélie and Louis embarked on an adventure they did not choose, but they were not left unprepared. Their faith, especially their habit of paying close attention to God's will, formed the foundation of their marriage and led to happiness and holiness. Like them, may we also listen for God's still, small voice (see 1 Kgs 19:11–12). And may this voice point us to God's plan for our lives, a plan greater than anything we could have chosen for ourselves!

## Spiritual Practice

1. In what ways has God surprised you in your marriage? What unexpected adventures have you experienced? When have these providential twists

and turns turned out better than what you might have chosen?

2. Discuss some decisions you have made in your marriage when you did not pray first and try to listen to God's will. Have there been times when one or both of you chose something that seemed out of line with God's will for your marriage? How did it impact you as a couple?

3. Consider some ways you would like to serve God in the future. Take some time to pray for God's guidance.

## Closing Prayer

Dear God, thank you for the wonders of your plan for our lives. We ask you for the grace to confidently believe the Word of God once spoken to the prophet Jeremiah: "For I know well the plans I have in mind for you— oracle of the LORD—plans for your welfare and not for woe, so as to give you a future of hope" (29:11). Amen.

# Holy Examples

## Opening Prayer

### Prayer of Spouses
### to Saints Louis and Zélie Martin

Saints Louis and Zélie Martin,
today we turn to you in prayer.
By fulfilling the duties of your state in life
and practicing the evangelical virtues
as spouses and as parents,
you have modeled for us
an exemplary Christian life.
May the example
of your unwavering trust in God

and your constant willingness to surrender
all the joys, the trials,
the sorrows and the sufferings
that filled your life
encourage us to persevere
in our daily challenges
and to remain in joy and Christian hope.
Amen.

Within fifteen years of marrying, Zélie and Louis had nine children. Just as they mastered the arts of lacework and watchmaking, the couple began to master a far more important art: parenting. Their goal was not "children who would stay in the Church" or "children who would be successful or good athletes." Rather, they desired children who would simply give themselves entirely to God's kingdom. Their marital mission was nothing less than to raise saints. With God's grace, Zélie and Louis seem to have been quite successful in their endeavor. All five of their daughters—Marie, Pauline, Léonie, Celine, and Thérèse—entered religious life. And, as if this were not enough, Thérèse is now a canonized saint, and Léonie is up for beatification. But how did Zélie and Louis raise such holy children? Their parenting can be summed up by two principles: example and persistent trust. Today we'll look at the power of their exemplary life, and tomorrow we will examine their persistent trust.

One could say that the Martins were like "supermodels," not in the fashion-world sense, but in the sense that they were exemplary Christian disciples. Their lives demonstrated the truth that a credible witness to the Gospel can be more compelling than any other form of evangelization. For instance, the Martins excelled in the virtue of hospitality and the Works of Mercy. Before they had children of their own, the couple informally fostered an orphan until parents could be found. During their child-raising years, Louis happened to see a man he knew in public who had lost his job and whose family was living in poverty. This man was by no means a close friend of the Martins. Nevertheless, Zélie welcomed the family into their home, and Louis sought a job for the unemployed father. Another time, when Louis saw a beggar in need, he bought shoes for him and invited him home to eat dinner with the Martin family. Louis then advocated for the man until he was given a bed to convalesce.

Despite their busy life, Zélie and Louis consistently demonstrated an acute awareness for those in need. In some cases, the Martins even took pains to advocate legally for those in desperate situations. In one instance, Zélie became aware of the misdeeds of two schoolteachers who wore a religious habit without Church sanction.

Zélie uncovered that these imposter religious sisters were neglecting and starving a little girl under their care. She immediately advocated for the child, and when the women refused to admit their wrongdoing, Zélie got the police involved. The women then began a public smear campaign against Zélie that was embarrassing for the entire family. Finally, the truth came to light, and the girl who had been under the women's care found a good home.

The Martins also set an example for their children and others with their devotion and love for God. They consistently rose early and walked to a 5:30 a.m. daily Mass. Louis never opened his jeweler's shop on Sundays, even though this was often the busiest business day. The couple also assiduously and joyfully observed all the liturgical days of fasting and penance, which were more numerous at the time. Their letters reveal another key feature of their piety—Louis and Zélie prayed often for their children's salvation, sanctification, and vocations. Their prayers for their children were not general and vague. Rather, the married couple devoted much consideration to each child's personal development. In her letters, Zélie in particular demonstrated a profound psychological understanding of each of her children.

Just as the Martins' example of holiness was surely inspiring to their children, it can also inspire us. Louis and Zélie shared God's love with those around them because they recognized that their responsibility to serve others extended beyond the walls of their home. Their motherly and fatherly hearts were expansive enough to love each of their children as well as those in need around them. We too can extend our hearts to love, even when it's frustrating or inconvenient. For example, many of us know children in our neighborhoods who have little to no supervision in the afternoons. Providing a warm home with supervision and snacks is one way to exercise hospitality. For some of these children, an extra adult investing in and caring about them can make all the difference. Taking in foster children is another option for those couples that are able.

Louis and Zélie also regularly demonstrated that their first priority was their faith. Married couples can do this in many simple ways that can leave a lasting impression on others. It's particularly important for couples that have children. Like Louis and Zélie, we can show others that God comes first in many ways. For example, every Sunday we can choose to put aside paperwork and rework our chore schedules so that we can truly rest with our families. Even in the midst of busyness, we can choose to spend time praying the Rosary as a family or reading Scripture with our spouse or children. Following the example of Louis and Zélie is not impossible. With

God's grace, we can put God first in our families and show our spouses, children, and those around us radical hospitality. Like Louis and Zélie, with hearts full of love, may we be holy examples to our families and to those around us.

## Spiritual Practice

1. We can't all be runway supermodels, but every one of us can be supermodels of virtue. What is one way Saints Louis and Zélie have inspired you to be a better example for your spouse, your children, or the wider community?

2. In an effort to encourage one another, discuss one way your spouse is a holy example to you. Give your spouse concrete examples of times you have been inspired by his or her example.

3. Resolve to try one way to be a better example for your spouse, children, or your community.

## Closing Prayer

Holy Trinity, help us to see better the many ways that we can be "supermodels" of virtue for one another. Please give us each the courage to become better examples for our spouse, our children, and for the people around us. Amen.

# Long-Suffering Trust

## Opening Prayer

### Psalm 130

Out of the depths I call to you, LORD;
    LORD, hear my cry!
May your ears be attentive
    to my cry for mercy.
If you, LORD, keep account of sins,
    LORD, who can stand?
But with you is forgiveness
    and so you are revered.
I wait for the LORD,
    my soul waits

and I hope for his word.
My soul looks for the LORD
    more than sentinels for daybreak.
More than sentinels for daybreak,
    let Israel hope in the LORD,
For with the LORD is mercy,
    with him is plenteous redemption,
And he will redeem Israel
    from all its sins.

Yesterday, we were inspired by Louis and Zélie's profound and joyful witness of Christian virtue. Today we look at their example of long-suffering, persistent trust in God. Sometimes we can be tempted to think that the saints were able to be holy because their lives were not difficult like ours. Nothing could be further from the truth. The Martins faced many struggles as tragedy after tragedy struck the family. Amid their difficulties, Louis and Zélie's response to suffering can inspire us to trust in God as they did. Their example helps us to believe that, with God's grace, our families can also thrive amid life's most challenging adversities.

One of the greatest sufferings that Louis and Zélie experienced was illness and death among their children. In fact, all their children at some point suffered life-threatening illnesses. While five of their children recovered, four did not. Zélie and Louis bore these losses nobly and abandoned themselves to God's will. Each time tragedy struck, the couple demonstrated confidence in God in their letters to one other and to relatives. Despite their grief, the couple continued to be open to life and to God's will, even when the deaths they were grieving came one after the other. Zélie, for instance, had to endure the death of her father, Isidore, just two weeks after the death of her son, Marie-Joseph-Jean-Baptiste.

The Martins also endured something many parents can relate to—the cross of difficult, badly behaved children. In fact, their two children who would later be recognized by the Church for their holiness were also the cause of suffering for their parents. Their overly sensitive youngest, Thérèse, was prone to temper tantrums. And, Léonie, for a variety of reasons, was so badly behaved that she was expelled from a convent school. Zélie explained what happened in one of her letters: "It was necessary to separate her from the other children. As soon as she is with companions, she seems to lose control of herself, and you never saw anything like her unruliness. Well, I have no longer any hope of changing her nature save by a miracle."[46] Despite the apparent hopelessness of Léonie's situation, God listened to Zélie's desperate prayers. While Léonie tried to join religious life three times, she finally found a home with the Visitation sisters. After she died, the Visitation sisters began receiving requests from all over the world for Léonie's intercession, and her beatification process has been initiated. With the help of God's grace, the Martins' persistent love for their children, despite the difficulties, helped their children to overcome their struggles.

In addition to facing many deaths, the Martin family also experienced great physical suffering. In 1865 Zélie discovered a glandular swelling in her breast that was accompanied by pain, numbness, and an inability to nurse. Imagine being unable to nurse in a world without formula or baby bottles! She carried this heavy cross for years and had to send several of her children away to be nursed. Due to the neglect of one wet nurse, her eighth child died. Thérèse also was entrusted to a wet nurse for fifteen long months. Zélie suffered greatly in this time, only able to see her daughter on visits to the nurse's home. It must have broken Zélie's heart to see Thérèse treat the wet nurse as if she were her mother. More than the death of her children and the pain of cancer, this pain must have brought the greatest grief to this noble woman. In 1876 the swelling in her breast increased, and Zélie was diagnosed with a tumor. She died the next year. Thérèse, her youngest daughter, was only four years old.

We all have crosses to bear in our marriages. Everyone experiences suffering and sorrow, no matter what we see on their social media accounts. The difference between overcoming these sorrows or being broken by them lies in how we bear our crosses. Do we carry them heroically or do we whine and complain and advertise our great suffering to gain attention and praise from those around us? Of course, it's not wrong to let God and other people know that we need assistance when we are suffering. In fact, many of the psalms are just that—pleas for help in the face of trials. Zélie and Louis model for us how to allow the suffering in our lives to lead us to trust and steadfast hope in the Lord. Jesus never promised an easy life. He said instead, "Whoever wishes to come after me must deny himself, take up his cross, and follow me" (Mt 16:24). The good news is that while we are guaranteed suffering when we take up our crosses, we are also guaranteed eternal joy in heaven because we are following Jesus. May God give us the grace to hold onto that hope in all we do.

*Saints Louis and Zélie Martin, pray for us!*

## Spiritual Practice

1. What crosses are you more apt to complain about? What kinds of crosses are you disposed to accept heroically? Discuss this with your spouse, and compare differences and similarities. How do you

feel called to support your spouse in carrying the crosses that seem most difficult for him or her?

2. Read and reflect on this poem written by Saint Thérèse de Lisieux when she was a child. It conveys the spirit of the Martin home, so full of joy yet also well-acquainted with the bitterness of suffering:

> *O, how I love the memories that cling*
> *To blessed childhood days!*
> *To guard the flower of my innocence*
> *My God o'er spread me with love.*[47]

3. What is one cross, big or small, that you and your spouse are bearing now? How can you both support one another in carrying that cross with joy and confident trust in the Lord? Resolve to imitate the Martins in one concrete way as you carry this cross together.

## Closing Prayer

Jesus, please give us the same radical trust that buoyed the Martins' faith throughout their trouble-filled life. Help us to find your peace amid all difficulty. Amen.

# Conclusion

# Make Love Your Aim

## Opening Prayer

### A Prayer for Our Marriage

Heavenly Father, we thank you for the gift of our marriage and for the many joys and blessings that have come to us through this vocation. Help us to appreciate one another's uniqueness and to overcome differences and difficulties with the help of your grace. Through the intercession of Saint Joseph, we ask you to protect our marriage from the evils of this world. Grant us the power to forgive each other when we have been hurt and the humility to ask for forgiveness when we have caused pain. Unite us in the love of your son, Jesus, that we may be a sign of your love to the world. Lead us each day to ever-greater holiness so that we may spend eternal life with you. Amen.

A s these days of reflection come to a close, we hope these married saints have inspired you to answer the call to sanctity in your marriage and have provided more concrete means to answer that call. Moses, the great patriarch of our faith, gave these final words of encouragement to the Israelites before they crossed the Jordan into the Promised Land. His speech, given to a people embarking on an adventure they could neither fathom nor predict, also applies to the journey of holiness in marriage:

> For this command which I am giving you today is not too wondrous or remote for you. It is not in the heavens, that you should say, "Who will go up to the heavens to get it for us and tell us of it, that we may do it?" Nor is it across the sea, that you should say, "Who will cross the sea to get it for us and tell us of it, that we may do it?" No, it is something very near to you, in your mouth and in your heart . . .
>
> See, I have today set before you life and good, death and evil. If you obey the commandments of the LORD, your God, which I am giving you today, loving the LORD, your God, and walking in his ways, and keeping

his commandments, statutes and ordinances, you will live and grow numerous, and the LORD, your God, will bless you in the land you are entering to possess. (Dt 30:11–16)

The way of holiness in the vocation of marriage is not far above us or off in the distance, but in our mouths and on our hearts—in God's word and in his commands.

What are the Lord's commands? Doubtless, the Ten Commandments. But God's commandment can also be summed up in Moses' words: "Hear, O Israel! The LORD is our God, the LORD alone! Therefore, you shall love the LORD, your God, with your whole heart, and with your whole being, and with your whole strength" (Dt 6:4–5). In the Gospel of John, Christ reiterates this command to love God with one's entire being, "This is my commandment: love one another as I love you. No one has greater love than this, to lay down one's life for one's friends" (Jn 15:12–13). In the lives of the married saints, we see this command lived out with heroic love. Blessed Frédéric Ozanam's life motto sums up how he made this command the center of his life: "Make love your aim!"

Marriage is not simple. At times your marriage may not seem anywhere close to the highlights of the married saints' lives. But every married couple faces hardship, and the married saints show us how to remain close to God in the midst of inevitable struggle. Christ calls married couples to follow him and to lay down our lives for one another and he will provide the grace necessary. Saint Paul wrote to the Corinthians that, while most things pass away, love remains (see 1 Cor 13:13). We are called in marriage to create, first and foremost, places where others can see the fruitful, life-giving love between a man and a woman that points toward God above all else. The story of each marriage is meant to be the story of a journey toward God.

Unfortunately, as may be obvious by now, these thirty days of reflections have not provided any magic formulas. The creativity of the Holy Spirit is endless so there's no fixed mold that married couples can strive to fit. The lives of the married saints are varied and each journey unique. Some were kings and others poor farmers. Some raised a gaggle of kids and others were childless. Some had relatively harmonious marriages and others had very serious struggles. Some were martyred and others died of old age. One might ask, "Is there nothing that integrates these disparate lives under the canopy of sanctity?" The answer is love—each saint loved God and gave his or her will over to his mysterious plan. This is the thread that binds these lives together into one, exquisite tapestry of the communion of saints.

On this final day of your thirty-day journey with the saints, we want to thank and congratulate you for having given this time to each other and to the Lord. Hopefully, you've already seen growth in virtue as a result of this experience together. But don't stop here! Keep your momentum going on the way of this holy pilgrimage. Continue watering the seeds of holiness just a little each day. Soon they will blossom with the fruits of the Spirit and the joy that comes from the peace of Christ. Fueled by God's undying love and friendship, you can be sure that his grace will strengthen your marriage and encourage you both to continue to love and trust the Lord. God can do immeasurably more than you can ask or imagine—so ask and imagine! His grace is enough to help you reach heaven together. As you edify one other on the way to heaven, your own marriage will undoubtedly bring others to Christ as well. In the hands of the greatest Craftsman, your marriage can encourage discipleship in all you meet. Inspired by the examples and prayers of the married saints, may your marriage—now and in generations to come—serve as a beacon for all those who attempt to navigate the way to heaven on uncertain seas!

All you holy married saints, pray for us!

## Spiritual Practice

1. Which married saints over the last thirty days taught you the most about love? Discuss and give

some examples. Resolve to imitate some of these saints by way of concrete actions.

2. Which of the married saints would be a strong intercessor for continued growth in holiness for you and your family? Why? Choose one or two saints as patron saints for your family.

3. Choose a way to celebrate the married saints in your home in the coming weeks, perhaps by creating a home altar or hosting an event (e.g., a trivia night or a family party). If you have children, let them participate in your brainstorming.

## Closing Prayer

Heavenly Father, grant us each day the grace to continue to grow in love so that one day we may become married saints! We call upon the intercession of all the saints in heaven to pray for our family's safety, health, and holiness. Amen.

# Notes

1. John Paul II, "Homily at the Beatification of Luigi Beltrame Quattrocchi and Maria Corsini," October 21, 2001. http://w2.vatican.va/content/john-paul-ii/en/homilies/2001/documents/hf_jp-ii_hom_20011021_beltrame-quattrocchi.html.

2. Ferdinand Holböck, *Married Saints and Blesseds Through the Centuries* (San Francisco: Ignatius Press, 2001), 195.

3. Pope Leo XIII, *Iucunda Semper Expectatione*, September 8, 1894. http://w2.vatican.va/content/leo-xiii/en/encyclicals/documents/hf_l-xiii_enc_08091894_iucunda-semper-expectatione.html.

4. Pope Pius XI, *Casti Connubii*, December 31, 1930. http://www.vatican.va/content/pius-xi/en/encyclicals/documents/hf_p-xi_enc_19301231_casti-connubii.html.

5. Paolino Beltrame Quattrocchi, "Son Tells How His Parents Raced Each Other to Sanctity: Memories of Father Paolino Beltrame Quattrocchi," zenit.org, October 21, 2001. https://zenit.org/articles/son-tells-how-his-parents-raced-each-other-to-sanctity/

6. Ibid.

7. *The Augustinian Manual, Comprising, a "Practical Prayer Book,"* by an Augustinian father Dublin: H.H. Gill and Song, 1885), 409 (modernized).

8. "Es el bien más grande de la Iglesia." See: Pope John Paul II, *Carta del Santo Padre Juan Pablo Ii a Los Sacerdotes con Ocasión del Jueves Santo,* March 25, 1982. https://w2.vatican. va/content/john-paul-ii/es/letters/1982/documents/hf_jp-ii_ let_19820325_sacerdoti-giovedi-santo.html.

9. Giuliana Pelucchi, *Saint Gianna Beretta Molla: A Woman's Life,* 1922–1962 trans. Paul Duggan (Boston: Pauline Books & Media, 2002), ix.

10. Ibid., 30.

11. Translated from Pope Paul VI, Angelus Message, September 23, 1973, https://w2.vatican.va/content/paul-vi/it/ angelus/1973/documents/hf_p-vi_ang_19730923.html.

12. Pelucchi, *Saint Gianna,* 30.

13. Ibid., 43.

14. Ibid., 44.

15. Ibid., 45–6.

16. Ibid., 54.

17. Ibid., 71–2.

18. Ibid., 66.

19. Ibid., 67.

20. Ibid., 68.

21. Ibid., 30.

22. Franz Jägerstätter, *Letters and Writings from Prison,* ed. Erna Putz, trans. Robert A. Krieg (Maryknoll, New York: Orbis Books, 2009), 182.

23. Ibid., 243.

24. Ibid. 130.

25. Ibid., 97–8.

26. Ibid., 127.

27. Monsignor Baunard, *Ozanam in His Correspondence* (New York: Benzinger Brothers, c. 1910), 279. (adapted)

28. Ibid., 257.

29. Ibid., 97.

30. Ibid., 178.

31. Ibid., 186.

32. Ibid.

33. Ibid.

34. Saint Augustine of Hippo, *The Confessions of St. Augustine* (Garden City, New York: International Collectors Library, 1900), 48. (adapted)

35. Ibid., 49.

36. Ibid., 80.

37. Ibid., 92.

38. Ibid., 83.

39. Ibid., 160.

40. Ibid., 161.

41. Ibid., 178.

42. Ibid., 180.

43. Pierre-Marie Grégoire, *Maidens of Hallowed Names* (New York: P.J. Kenedy, 1881), 365. (adapted)

44. Philip Schaff and Henry Wace, eds., *A Select Library of the Nicene and Post-Nicene Fathers of the Christian Church,*

Second Series, vol. 6 (Buffalo: The Christian Literature Co., 1894), 402. (adapted)

45. Ibid., 402–3.

46. See the letter from Mme Martin to Mme Guérin CF 117 - June 1, 1874. http://www.archives-carmel-lisieux.fr/english/ carmel/index.php/mme-martin/1306-lettre-de-mme- \martin-cf-117-1er-juin-1874.

47. See The Canticle of Celine, PN 18, http://www.archives-carmel-lisieux.fr/carmel/index.php/pn-18.

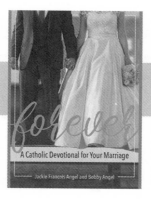

A Catholic Devotional for Your Marriage

Jackie Francois Angel and Bobby Angel

Discover new meaning, joy, and practical tips for your marriage as you pray through this six-week devotional. Rooted in the profound wisdom of Saint John Paul II's theology of the body, each day of reflections and prayer will guide you to grow closer to God—and to one another.

By Jackie Francois Angel and Bobby Angel

0-8198-2743-6
$15.95
paperback,  176 pages

**auline**
BOOKS & MEDIA

A mission of the Daughters of St. Paul

As apostles of Jesus Christ, evangelizing today's world:

We are CALLED to holiness
by God's living Word and Eucharist.

We COMMUNICATE the Gospel message
through our lives and through all
available forms of media.

We SERVE the Church
by responding to the hopes and needs
of all people with the Word of God,
in the spirit of St. Paul.

For more information visit our Web site:
www.pauline.org.

## BOOKS & MEDIA

The Daughters of St. Paul operate book and media centers at the following addresses. Visit, call, or write the one nearest you today, or find us at www.paulinestore.org.

**CALIFORNIA**
3908 Sepulveda Blvd, Culver City, CA 90230 — 310-397-8676
3250 Middlefield Road, Menlo Park, CA 94025 — 650-562-7060

**FLORIDA**
145 S.W. 107th Avenue, Miami, FL 33174 — 305-559-6715

**HAWAII**
1143 Bishop Street, Honolulu, HI 96813 — 808-521-2731

**ILLINOIS**
172 North Michigan Avenue, Chicago, IL 60601 — 312-346-4228

**LOUISIANA**
4403 Veterans Memorial Blvd, Metairie, LA 70006 — 504-887-7631

**MASSACHUSETTS**
885 Providence Hwy, Dedham, MA 02026 — 781-326-5385

**MISSOURI**
9804 Watson Road, St. Louis, MO 63126 — 314-965-3512

**NEW YORK**
115 E. 29th Street, New York City, NY 10016 — 212-754-1110

**SOUTH CAROLINA**
243 King Street, Charleston, SC 29401 — 843-577-0175

**VIRGINIA**
1025 King Street, Alexandria, VA 22314 — 703-549-3806

**CANADA**
3022 Dufferin Street, Toronto, ON M6B 3T5 — 416-781-9131

¡También somos su fuente para libros,
videos y música en español!